Weigh Less Naturally

HINKLER
BOOKS

First published in 2002 by Hinkler Books Pty Ltd
17-23 Redwood Drive
Dingley Victoria 3172 Australia
www.hinklerbooks.com

Text © Karen Hobbs 2002
Design © Hinkler Books Pty Ltd

Reprinted 2002 (twice), 2003 (three times)

ISBN 1 86515 501 2

Design: Sam Grimmer
Editorial: Writers Reign
Typesetting: Midland Typesetters
Printed and bound in Australia

Acknowledgements

I thank the Lord for the gifts he has placed in me, for the passion he has given me to reach out and help as many people as possible come to the realisation that life does not have to be full of 'starvation and deprivation'. I am so thankful for the doors of opportunity he opened so that this book could be published.

There are many people to whom I give heartfelt thanks. These people have encouraged me and enrich my life so much.

My special husband Wayne, who walked into my life during the production of this book - you are awesome, and your support and encouragement mean the world to me. Thank you for being a great 'gourmet guinea pig' when I experimented with the recipes.

My wonderful children for putting up with me during the stressful times and not giving up on me and the dreams I have.

Gary, who for many years supported me in my endeavour to follow my dreams, and who spent countless hours on the computer and balancing the books.

My best friend Lorral for helping me out in the kitchen all those times.

To all my beautiful, wonderful members who inspire me to continue.

And a big thank you to all the guys at Hinkler and Brigid James who have taken my dream and brought it to you in this book.

May this book bless you and help you achieve your dream!

This book is lovingly dedicated to my beautiful children Tyler and Melinda and to all my special members who encouraged me to share my love and passion for helping others by writing this book.

Important

It is advisable before starting any weight loss program to consult your doctor. If any problems develop or you become pregnant, seek medical advice before continuing with this weight loss program.

The recipes in this book have been created by the author. Any similarity to existing recipes is purely coincidental.

Share your success story with us. We would love to hear how you have gone in your endeavours to lose weight on this program and how you have enjoyed the recipes.

Write your story and forward it to:

Weigh Less Naturally
PO Box 211
Nobby Beach
Queensland, Australia 4218
or email
karen@weighless.com.au

We look forward to hearing from you soon.

If you would like more information on meetings check out Karen Hobbs's website on www.weighless.com.au or phone (07) 5575 1777.

If you would like Karen to speak at your group meeting or conference please contact her at the above address.

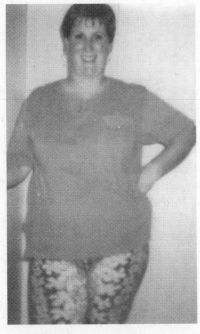 

Author Karen Hobbs before (left) and after (right) her Weigh Less Naturally program.

Endorsements

Five years ago a ball of energy walked into my office and I had a sense that here was a lady who knew how to get things done.

My first instincts proved to be accurate. During this time I have been impressed and amazed at the profound changes she has been able to make in the quality of people's lives through her weight loss philosophies.

On a professional level her guidance and motivation has made the difference in the health and well-being of many of my patients.

I have been fortunate to sample many delicious, healthy and exciting new recipes and at many a dinner party have witnessed a concerned diner reassured by the words 'Don't worry, it is one of Karen's recipes'.

Karen Hobbs has such a wealth of knowledge and a real passion to communicate it that this book simply had to written. Her program is about a lifestyle and an attitude, not just a diet and this is evident in this book.

Personally and professionally I recommend this book to you. Read it, enjoy the recipes, be inspired and embrace the lifestyle it promotes.

Dr John Evans
MSc

As a General Practitioner interested in the preventative health of my patients I am much aware of the health risks associated with obesity and excess weight. Encouraging patients about loss and the benefits to their health is one of the most challenging roles of a General Practitioner.

So many of my patients have taken on this challenge under the guidance of Karen Hobbs and her Weigh Less Naturally program. She has successfully motivated and encourage my patients, not just for a temporary weight loss program but for a lifetime of healthy eating, thus ensuring a new zest for life, a renewed energy and overall improvement in their health.

Karen manages to get these patients motivated and excited about their health. They report to me about how well they feel, how much they are eating (often much more than ever before), and how proud they are of themselves as the weight falls off. Karen has truly made an important change in their lives.

I'd highly recommend anyone take the challenge, listen to what Karen has to say and change their life.

Dr. Peter Morely
M.B. Ch.B.
Burleigh Family Medical Practice

Contents

Welcome to a new lifestyle

Karen's story

To change the way you look and feel, you need to change something you are doing, and change it forever.

This has become my motto. For twenty years I had unsuccessfully tried diets with the result that my weight was like a yoyo. Even though I made some changes, they only lasted while I was on the latest diet craze. You name it, I tried it! But soon enough I would always fall back to my old habits. Why? Those diets were full of deprivation and starvation.

Six years ago I finally realised that the answer was simple - a balanced diet that is flexible and enjoyable. With my passion for food, and the knowledge I had gained from twenty years of dieting, Weigh Less Naturally was created.

Today I spend a lot of my time playing in the kitchen creating recipes. I am constantly updating my knowledge of nutrition and exercise. Most importantly, I help other people to achieve their dreams of losing weight, eating well and being healthier and happier.

I believe in everything in moderation (this means that there are no 'naughty foods' so ban the word 'diet' right now). I personally managed to fit three 60 gram Mars bars and a couple of glasses of wine into my week as I shed my 31 kilograms. Today I maintain that weight loss and enjoy a happy, healthy lifestyle. Now my days include plenty of great tasting food that is suitable for all the family and good enough to serve up at any dinner party. You can eat pastries, pies and desserts and lose weight by living the Weigh Less Naturally way.

Learning to cook great low-fat food is the missing key for many of us. In my case I was good at following a diet for about a month, but I would then become tired with the same boring diet food. That boredom may be familiar to you, and it usually leads to falling off the wagon, feeling a failure and dropping out. So the circle of dieting goes on!

Make a decision right now and decide that this is the last time you are going to lose weight.

Testimonial

'I lost 45 kilos and went from size 24 to size 10.'

It's funny how weight seems to creep on you, and then one day you get a 'wake-up call'.

I had always weighed 57 kilograms. Then I met my husband, life was wonderful, and there were nights of dining out or eating takeaway. Two children later I was shopping for a pair of shorts one day and was horrified to find that the only size that would fit was size 24! I knew I had to do something about it there and then.

That day I saw an advertisement for Weigh Less Naturally. I looked at that ad for five days until I plucked up the courage to ring Karen. I joined that night and weighed in at 103 kilograms - I had a lot of work ahead of me!

I found the food program very easy to follow, with lots to eat and great recipes that the whole family would eat. Before I knew it I had lost 13 kilograms in just twelve weeks. The weeks started to add up and one year later I was walking into shops buying size 10 clothes. My husband loves the new me and my children now have trouble keeping up with their fit, slim and healthy mum. The only problem I have now is that people who have not seen me for a while walk straight by me in the street, because they don't recognise me.

Losing the weight gave me so much more self-esteem and confidence. I even entered and won a national weight loss competition!

Stacey Hall, 'Slimmer of the Year 2001' - *Slimming Magazine*

'I am now a size 10 and love shopping for clothes, knowing they will fit me and look good.'

I have always been a healthy weight, but in the span of a year I managed to pile on 15 kilograms. I really didn't notice the change until one day I looked in the mirror and was shocked at what I saw.

I knew that I had to do something. I had heard about the Weigh Less Naturally program and decided to give it a try.

The food was so good and the portions were so generous that I found it an easy program to stick to. I was also able to eat the foods I loved, and dine out regularly.

I do not feel that I am on a 'diet'; I have made a lifestyle choice. I feel much healthier and fitter now - it is hard to believe that I was once struggling to get into a size 14-16 dress. I am now a size 10 and love shopping for clothes knowing they are going to fit and look good.

Melissa Silkman

'I have lost 22.6 kilograms and I could not be happier.'

As a mother and a wife, life often seems to revolve around food – preparing it, eating it, serving it and worrying about it. This is not a good thing for someone with a weight problem.

Then my sister told me about a group that gave out recipes each week. Her favourite recipe is Singapore Noodles. The beauty about this recipe is that it takes less time to prepare than stopping at the local fish and chip shop. My list of favourites goes on and on, and most nights I can come home and have dinner on the table within a half an hour.

The added bonus with Karen's group is the time she put into her recipes to help us enjoy our weight loss. I love to cook, and even the food bill has decreased since we now limit our main meal to 100 grams protein with many vegetables.

I was invited to a lunch one day and we had to take along a plate of food so I brought the Salmon Crepe Stack. Many people raved about the dish and when I told them about the group they were all stunned.

Once when I made Spaghetti Bolognaise, my husband served the meal and wondered why I was upset with him because there was still food left in the saucepan. I told him that the recipe was for four people – so there shouldn't have been any left-overs.

The serves are plentiful and the food is very nice. The added bonus is that I have lost 22.6 kilograms over ten months, and I could not be happier.

Gail Szandurski

'I lost 24 kilos and my husband jokes "We've never eaten so well!"'

Seven months after going to my first Weigh Less Naturally meeting, I had lost 15 kilograms and reached my goal weight of 75 kilograms.

Neither Karen nor I wanted to set an unreasonable goal. I had tried to lose weight many times before with different plans and although I had managed once to get down to 70 kilograms on one program, but I couldn't keep it off.

Now, after fifteen months on Karen's program my weight is at a comfortable 66 kilograms, a total loss of 24 kilograms. I have maintained that loss for two years.

My husband jokes that we've never eaten so well—but it's perfectly true. Karen's recipes are really interesting and I find myself tackling dishes I would never have dreamt of before.

I bless the day I met Karen and I can't thank her enough for what she has helped me to achieve!

Jean Rees-Osborne

'I lost 30 kilos and went from size 20 to size 10 – and still ate my favourite chocolate!'

I moved from the country to the Gold Coast and had no friends at the time and felt incredibly lonely. Food became my comfort and best friend. I was so tired and run down all the time, and started bursting out of my clothes. I had gone from size 14 to size 20 in two years. I knew I had to do something about it there and then.

I rang around many weight loss centres trying to find one that suited my budget, and found Weigh Less Naturally.

It is amazing how much food you can eat, how you can still enjoy your favourite treats and still lose weight! I learnt how to cook tasty low-fat food. I have now lost 30 kilograms and maintained that loss for two years. I am full of energy and confidence, and just love being able to wear modern clothes again.

I feel like a new person.

Marnie Croft (See page 206.)

'We lost 52 kilos between us – Graeme shrunk from size XXXL to size L and I went from size 18 to size 10!'

As a plumber, Graeme found the extra weight he was carrying around debilitating to say the least. He was self-conscious and reluctant to join me swimming, lacking any energy to do anything. I was a severe cholesterol sufferer and required medication.

With Weigh Less Naturally, we were able to change our lives and manage all of these problems. With Karen's guidance I have been able to maintain low cholesterol readings without medication. I now play competition squash twice a week and walk. Graeme has become unstoppable.

We gained the support we needed to keep us on track. We love our new healthy eating plan. The food is enough to satisfy the whole family, including our two teenage children. We have found a good balance between living a healthy life, having fun and happiness.

We have lost 52 kilograms between us. The part which was the most fun was replacing our large clothes.

Sheryl Kirby (See page 206.)

'I lost 23 kilos in eight months and went from size 18 to size 10!'

Turning forty and being fat was a terrifying thought. I had longed to be slim for years and I just could not get the motivation to do it until I joined Weigh Less Naturally.

Thanks to Karen's support, and the Weigh Less Program, I am now a size 8-10. I now know what it is like to be able to go into a shop and pick up clothing in modern styles that I like – and not just the styles that fit!

I am a very different person now I have lost the weight, and I have a lot more confidence. I have now met and married the man of my dreams and I know I will never return to size 18 again!

April Mills

'Weigh Less Naturally has certainly changed my life for the better.'

At 4'10' tall, 76 kilos was too much to be carrying around everyday. My doctor told me I had to have a double knee replacement and would need to lose some weight to help with my recovery.

Joining Weigh Less Naturally was the best decision I ever made. In six months I lost 17 kilograms, and feel 100 per cent better. I have more energy and motivation, and my knees have felt the benefit.

After meeting Karen I was inspired by her dedication and patience, and also the way in which she presented the recipes. They are simple to prepare, and the whole family enjoyed the meals.

The program is so easy to follow – Weigh Less Naturally has certainly changed my life for the better.

Doreen Keech

'Weigh Less Naturally is a part of my life now'

I tried a number of weight loss clubs, but while I lost the weight I never managed to keep it off – I would lose interest. I joined Weigh Less Naturally in August 1999, and have managed to lose my weight and keep it off since then.

After having my first child (my daughter) I put on 18 kilograms. I tried all the fad diets, but as soon as I went back to eating normally I would put the weight back on! When I was pregnant with my second child, I put on weight again, and with the birth of my son I gained 12 kilograms. I joined Weigh Less Naturally with a weight of 62.7 kilograms and I now weigh 56 kilograms. I know that 6 kilograms does not seem a lot for some people to lose but to me it meant that all my clothes did not fit and I felt frumpy.

I have now maintained this weight for the last three years and have never felt better. I now have a high self-esteem and a healthy lifestyle. My family enjoys the recipes, which is great as I do not have to cook separate meals.

Weigh Less Naturally is now a part of my life.

Sue Raven

Stacey Hall, 'Slimmer of the Year 2001', before and after the Weigh Less Naturally program.

Understanding The Weigh Less Naturally Program

Live the dream

Congratulations! You have taken the first step to losing weight and having a healthy lifestyle by purchasing this book. Now you need the vision to know where it is you want to go. If you do not know where you are going, how are you ever going to get there?

Give yourself some quiet time right now to think about just what it is that you want to achieve. Your dream may be to fit into your jeans; or to go into a shop and buy the clothes that you like, and not just the ones that fit you. Perhaps your dream is just to be able to walk up stairs without huffing and puffing, or play with your children. When you have decided what it is that you want to achieve, write it down in the space below.

This will serve as a tool to help you keep your focus while you are travelling the road to becoming a healthier and slimmer person. Make sure you reread your vision or dream daily.

_____

_____

_____

_____

_____

Date _____

Now you need to set specific goals that will enable you to reach your dream.

Karen Hobbs has been running the Weigh Less Naturally food program successfully for many years. The program was developed using calorie measurements. Readers who would prefer to use a kilojoule count can use the simple conversion of 1 calorie to 4 kilojoules.

Making a commitment— setting goals

Remember that every choice you make brings about a result. What result do you want to see? Think about the result before you make a decision and then make a commitment.

You need to set yourself goals as these will keep you motivated and moving in the right direction. Make sure that your goals are achievable and realistic - remember that it is easier to take lots of small steps than it is to take big ones! It is a common problem that people often try to lose too much weight at once, and become dispirited when they can't reach these unrealistic goals. Try not to think about any goals you may have failed to reach in the past; this is a new way of life and so you need to start afresh, with an open and positive mind.

Start small. Establish daily, weekly, monthly and yearly goals. For example, if you want to lose 25 kilograms, that seems like a very big target and can be daunting. But break the goal down. If you manage to lose just 2 kilograms each month, over a year that amounts to 24 kilograms.

That is an obtainable goal, and one that you can achieve while still enjoying the foods you like, such as chocolate or wine, in moderation.

You may like to embark on a new exercise program. Once again, start small. You could start off with a ten-minute walk each day and slowly build it up.

Write down your goals now!

_____

_____

_____

_____

_____

_____

_____

Look back at your goals regularly and update them as you succeed.

Success is in the planning

Now that you have a dream or vision of where you would like to be, and you have set your goals and decided to commit to achieving them, you need a basic food plan to get you there – a menu planner that will help you, with tips on how to be a smart shopper plus great recipes. That is what is in this book. The rest is up to you.

Learning to plan is something that all successful slimmers need to practise. Just a little organisation can go a long way towards good weight loss and permanent changes in your lifestyle.

I came to realise that in order to change the way I looked and felt I had to change some things in my life, because nothing happens without change. For years my excuse was that I was always too busy. I worked seventy hours a week in the hotel industry, and had a husband, two young children, a dog, two cats and a house and garden to care for. These were very hectic and crazy days. That busy kind of lifestyle is very common these days and it can be stressful. The important thing for you to remember is that you can be in control of your life, and you can succeed in your dreams, no matter how busy you are.

I decided to set aside a couple of hours once a week to cook food and freeze it so that I was not forced to buy take-away and fast food (which are loaded with fat) when I didn't have the time to cook a proper meal. Planning your meals makes life so much easier and can save you money.

Take a little time to think about the week ahead. Browse through the recipes in this book and choose what to make according to the time you have available. For example, if you are going to have a busy week at work, choose stir-fry recipes, or a quiche that you can make the night before. You could also double recipes so that you have plenty of leftovers to use for other meals. (You will notice this tactic is used in the 21-day plan on page 33.) By planning ahead you can make sure that you are making the most of all the recipes so that you are gaining variety and consuming good quantities of food each day. You can write out your shopping list and head off to the shops knowing exactly what you need.

Mistakes are opportunities in disguise

Everybody makes mistakes. Sometimes you might feel that you have overeaten, binged or lost the plot. You might feel disappointed, guilty and defeated. It is important to remember that everyone can relate to these feelings, and that you are not alone. Mistakes and failures feel awful at the time, but they are actually valuable experiences that you can learn from.

The most important thing to do is to recognise that mistakes are going to happen. Never allow yourself to think that you are hopeless or that you won't make it to your goal. You need to view the mistake in a positive light. Make it work for you instead of letting it drag you down.

Look carefully at what happened and try to find out why. Then plan a strategy that will prevent that situation recurring. This will not only help you to stay focused on the road to success, but will also help you to feel good about your mistakes and you will believe that you can achieve your dream.

Weigh Less Naturally food program

The Weigh Less Naturally food program is a well-balanced food plan which includes all the essential food groups that are needed for a healthy lifestyle – proteins, carbohydrates, fruits and dairy products.

In order to adopt a healthier lifestyle plan, you should understand why your body needs food from all the food groups. When your body lacks food, it automatically slows down your metabolic rate to conserve energy. So if your body is not getting enough of the right food it will not be functioning efficiently. For example, if you skip breakfast, you can slow down your metabolic rate by approximately 20 per cent. So don't be tempted to skip meals, and remember to start your body every morning with breakfast, even if it's only a quick fruit smoothie.

It is recommended that you keep a food diary and note down what you eat each day. It can be very easy to lose track of what you have consumed. A calorie counter is a useful tool and makes it much easier to maintain an accurate record.

Note: The program is based on a 1200-1500 calorie (4800-6000 kJ) count per day for women. Men and teenagers are permitted additional food serves. People wishing to maintain their weight can also have extra food serves (see page 37). The four food groups are:

Proteins

Proteins build and repair muscle, and are also needed for the body's organs, hormones, enzymes and antibodies (which fight infections). Lean red meat is rich in iron, zinc and vitamin B12.

If you use alternatives to red meat such as poultry, fish, eggs or legumes, then you have to ensure you get enough iron and zinc in your diet by eating wholemeal or wholegrain breads and cereals.

> In the recipes, all the meats are measured in uncooked measurements. Be careful to check that all visible fat has been removed. Take care when purchasing any type of minced meat that it is very lean.

Carbohydrates

Carbohydrates provide energy, valuable fibre, vitamins and minerals. They are mainly found in cereals, grains, fruit and vegetables. When carbohydrates are digested, they cause blood glucose to rise. Some are slow-acting (for example wholegrain or wholemeal breads, bran, oats, pasta and brown rice) and should be eaten regularly for even blood sugar levels. Fast-acting carbohydrates (for example those in white bread, rice cakes and low-fibre cereals) should be eaten in moderation.

An even distribution of carbohydrates throughout tne day is important.

Fruit

Fruits are full of valuable vitamins, minerals, natural sugars and fibre (the skin of the fruit is an excellent source of fibre). Fruit makes a great snack, a wonderful addition to desserts, and tastes good in yoghurt.

Fruit is an excellent food but you should limit yourself to one banana per day as they are higher in calories than other fruits.

Dairy

Dairy products are an excellent source of calcium. Calcium helps to ensure that you have strong, healthy bones and teeth.

If you have difficulty in consuming enough dairy products, try making a smoothie or custard with milk.

Optional Indulgences

When you are working to lose weight you still want to be able to enjoy a little of your favourite foods. When you follow the Weigh Less Naturally food program you have up to 250 calories (1000 kJ) each day that you can spend on whatever you would like. These are called Optional Indulgences.

These Optional Indulgences may be included in the recipes, for example you will see that sometimes sour cream or a little oil is used. They are also available to use up on your favourite foods such as wine, chocolate or crisps.

You can also use your Optional Indulgences to purchase other foods from the essential food groups such as extra carbohydrates, milk or fruit. You will notice this is done in some of the recipes.

The Optional Indulgences enable you to have small doses of your favourite treats while you lose weight. Complete deprivation can often lead to binge eating – the Weigh Less Naturally method means that you are more likely to stick to your goals and dreams.

Planning helps you to use the Optional Indulgences wisely. If you like a glass of wine each night with dinner, then you will need to plan for this. Know that each glass of wine will cost you 80 of your 250 Optional Indulgence calories per day, leaving you 170 Optional Indulgence calories to spend. If you are going out to dinner, think about saving up some Optional Indulgence calories for drinks and dessert. You can do this by saving up to 150 calories per day for six consecutive days, and then going out to dinner on the seventh day and enjoying the food knowing that you are still eating within the program.

Note: You cannot carry Optional Indulgences over from one week to the next.

Calorie counting

It is a good idea to purchase a calorie counter to keep on hand, so that you have some guide as to how many Optional Indulgence calories you spend on certain foods. I have provided a short list of examples to start you off.

Fats

Food	Serving	Calories	kJ
avocado	1 tablespoon	35	140
butter	1 teaspoon	35	140
cooking oil (eg olive, sesame)	1 teaspoon	45	180
cream pressure pack	2 tablespoons	35	140

Although you may want to ban fat from your diet, it is important to remember that some fats provide you with essential fatty acids and soluble vitamins. You should include some of these 'good' fats in your diet each day.

Condiments, sauces and flavourings

Food	Serving	Calories	kJ
chutney or relish	1 tablespoon	45	180
cocoa	1 tablespoon	25	100
cranberry sauce	1 tablespoon	45	180
golden or maple syrup	1 teaspoon	15	60
gherkin	1 tablespoon	45	180
honey	1 teaspoon	15	60
sugar	1 teaspoon	15	60
cornflour	1 tablespoon	40	160
custard powder	1 tablespoon	40	160
evaporated skim milk	125 ml	95	380
tomato sauce/ketchup	1 tablespoon	25	100

Snacks and drinks

Food	Serving	Calories	kJ
beer (low cal)	375 ml	100	400
carob chocolate	30 g	155	620
chocolate	1 g = 5 cal	20	
fun-size bars (eg Mars, Kit-Kat)	18–22 g	110	440
low-fat icecream	100 ml	70	280
popcorn (popped, no butter)	1 cup	55	220
potato crisps	25 g packet	125	500
pretzels	6 g (10 sticks)	25	100
sorbet (no-milk or fat)	100 ml	55	220
soya crisps	15 crisps	140	560
spirits	30 ml	65	260
vanilla icecream	100 ml	90	360
wine	1 glass	80	320
	(six glasses to a 750 ml bottle)		

Abbreviations

protein	PR
carbohydrate	CB
fruit	F
dairy	D

Conversion tables

Weights

30 g	1 oz
125 g	4 oz
250 g	8 oz
500 g	16 oz
1 kg	32 oz

Volume

30 ml	1 fl oz
125 ml	4 fl oz
250 ml	8 fl oz
500 ml	16 fl oz
1 litre	32 fl oz

Cups

¼ cup	65 ml	2 fl oz
½ cup	125 ml	4 fl oz
1 cup	250 ml	8 fl oz

Oven temperatures

170°C	325°F
180	350
200	400

Exact conversions are impossible to give so it is important to use either metric or imperial measure when following a recipe.

Daily food summary

The summary below provides a guide you can use to assess each recipe. This should be used in conjunction with the 21-day plan to help you to plan your meals according to your total food intake.

Food group	Number of servings women	Number of servings men and teenagers	Example of one serving
Protein	3-4	4-5	50 g (2 oz) lean cut beef, chicken, turkey, lamb, veal 40 g (1½ oz) bacon or pastrami 50 g (2 oz) tinned fish (in water or brine), fresh fish 25 g (1 oz) firm cheese (eg cheddar, blue, feta) 65 g (2 oz) cottage cheese 1 egg ½ cup baked bean 1 chicken sausage 100 g (3 oz) tofu
Carbohydrates	5	6-7	1 slice of bread 30-40 g (1 oz) in weight 30 g (1 oz) cereal 1/2 cup cooked pasta, rice, noodles, corn kernels 150 g (5 oz) potato
Fruit	3	3	one medium sized fruit (eg apple, orange, banana) 3 small fruits (eg kiwifruit, figs, plums) 1 cup of fresh fruit salad or berries ½ cup cooked or tinned fruit 30 g (1 oz) dried fruit 125 ml (4 fl oz) fruit juice
Dairy	4	4	125 ml (4 fl oz) low-fat milk 65 ml (2 fl oz) low-fat (no sugar added) yoghurt 1 low-fat cheese slice 65 ml (2 fl oz) evaporated skim milk
Water	6-8 glasses per day	6-8 glasses per day	

Free foods

The following foods may be consumed at any time. As long as they are consumed in moderation, they do not have to be restricted.

Drinks

Tea, coffee (or coffee substitutes), soda water, plain mineral water, diet soft drinks and diet cordials can all be consumed in moderation (although some of these contain sodium, which can make you retain fluids). Water is also an important part of any healthy diet. You should have at least 6–8 glasses each day. Water can assist with weight control, improve general health and is especially good for your kidneys. In summer try adding mint, cucumber or fruit to a glass for wonderful flavour. In winter drink water warm or hot with slices of lemon and/or orange.

Vegetables

All vegetables except for the limited starch vegetables (potato, sweet corn and sweet potato) are free so you can have as much as you like! Have at least 2½ cups of fresh, frozen or tinned vegetables each day. Make sure you have a variety of dark green and leafy vegetables (for example cabbage, spinach, broccoli, cauliflower, brussel sprouts) as they can help protect against cancer. Orange-yellow vegetables are excellent source of vitamin A. All vegetables are rich in vitamins, minerals and fibre.

Additives and flavourings

Artificial sweeteners, lemon and lime juice, baking powder/soda, yeast spreads cream of tartar, mustards, curry powder, non-stick cooking spray, jam (diet or 100 per cent fruit), oil-free dressings, essences such as vanilla, poppy or sesame seeds, gelatine and diet jellies, sauces such as black bean, hoi sin, soy, herbs, spices, stock powder, chilli, horseradish and wine (for cooking purposes only, not drinking!) are all free foods if consumed in moderation. These add great flavour to your food so it's worth experimenting with them as much as possible.

Dining out

Going out to dinner is an important part of social life. With some strategies, you can still succeed in your weight-loss goals while dining out.

There are hidden dangers when dining out as restaurant menus – unlike packaged food – do not provide a breakdown of the nutrition in each dish. Many foods can be full of hidden fats and carbohydrates. You may find it useful to use these hints as a guide when it comes to selecting what you wish to eat.

- Try to avoid going out feeling really hungry as you could lose control of what you eat.

- Don't skip meals on the day. Choose your food wisely so that you have plenty of Optional Indulgence calories up your sleeve.

- Ask for any sauces to be served on the side, so that you can control how much of the sauce you consume.

- Check the cooking method with your waiter, as your idea of 'pan fried' may be very different to the chef's.

- Skip dishes that are described as 'buttery', 'creamy', 'rich', 'deep-fried', 'scaloppine' and 'au gratin'.

- Have a plain bread roll instead of garlic bread. (One slice is 100 calories!)

- Order an entree size as your main meal, with a side serve of salad or vegetables.

- If there is a smorgasbord, fill up on clear soups and salads, leaving the hot buffet until last.

- Check the size of wine glasses. If they are big glasses, make sure you allow for this when counting your Optional Indulgences, or have a spritzer ($\frac{1}{2}$ wine and $\frac{1}{2}$ soda water).

What should you order?

If you are dining on Asian food, choose clear soups, steamed rice and dishes plentiful in vegetables. Beware of satay, coconut cream, fried foods and sweet and sour sauces.

If you are dining on Italian food, choose tomato or meat-based dishes.

If you are dining on Mexican food, burritos and enchiladas are a good choice, but you should ask for light sour cream on the side. Avoid nacho chips.

If you are dining on pizza, request less cheese and more vegetables. Choose chicken or seafood pizzas and avoid salami and sausage. Have a salad with the pizza.

Smart shopping

Most of us have to face the task of grocery shopping each week. Some people may find it an easy, comfortable experience. But for others, it may be a minefield, with temptation lurking around every corner. This temptation can be conquered with a little know-how.

- Never shop when you are tired, grumpy or hungry.

- Never let yourself snack or taste samples while shopping as this may tempt you to fill your trolley with items that you don't want or need. When your taste buds are aroused, you are more likely to purchase foods on a taste basis, which can be expensive as well as bad for your diet.

- Schedule shopping time when you are more likely to be relaxed as shopping while stressed can make you susceptible to eating triggers and fancy packaging. Try to plan your shopping times during the least hectic times of the week so that you are not in competition with other shoppers, but have enough time to shop calmly.

- Always shop with a list and only buy what is on the list. This way you will not be led astray by marketing ploys, displays or so-called 'bargain' bins.

- Shop along the walls of a supermarket before going up the aisles, as the outside walls generally contain fruits, vegetables and dairy products. Aisles usually contain foods that are higher in fat, and you may be distracted by the packaging.

- Familiarise yourself with the layout of the store so that you know where you are going and do not end up wandering aimlessly, scanning the shelves, which may encourage you to buy what you see and not what is on the list.

- Avoid going to a new supermarket while hungry or in a hurry.

- Select refrigerated and frozen items last. Generally frozen fruit and vegetables are actually picked during the peak season, then snap frozen so that all the nutrients are retained. Frozen fruit and vegetables are a great time saver if you are a busy person.

Product labels

Read labels carefully. There is often so much advertising on product labels that it can be difficult to find what they are telling you about the actual content of the product. Practise reading nutritional breakdowns at home so that when you are in the supermarket you know what to look for. Often the energy value (calorie count) will help you to decide what to buy. It is important to remember that every product is made up of something. If a product is high in energy, it may also be high in fat or sugar.

Be aware that the nutritional breakdown does not always reflect the size of the packet. Most products have a breakdown for servings of 30 grams or 100 grams, but the product may weigh 150 grams. Therefore you need to multiply the calories listed to get the nutritional breakdown of the product that you are actually buying. For example, if you have a chocolate bar that advertises that it has 150 calories per 100 grams, but the chocolate bar actually weighs 150 grams, the calorie count for the whole bar amounts to 225 calories, not 150.

Misleading advertising

'Lite' products

Many products advertise themselves as being 'Lite' or 'Light'. This does not necessarily mean that the product is light in calories, fat or sugar.

One member of Weigh Less Naturally once found a 'light' chocolate cake in the freezer at the supermarket. She compared it to the 'regular' brand chocolate cake by the same manufacturer. Both products had exactly the same calorie count. She telephoned the manufacturer and asked 'Why is it advertised as light?' The manufacturer replied 'It is lighter in colour than the regular brand'!

Always try to compare the calorie counts.

Cholesterol free

Cholesterol and fat are not the same thing. So when products are labelled 'cholesterol free' this does not mean that they are also fat free. For example, cooking oil can be cholesterol free but in fact may contain 100 per cent fat. However, cholesterol free is the healthier option so choose it when possible.

'Low-fat' and 'no fat' products

You should always check the sugar content and calorie count of products that advertise as 'low-fat' or 'no fat'. Every product is made up of something. It may have a high sugar content, and so is also high in calories.

Low-fat yoghurt is a good example. Some low-fat brands have up to seven teaspoons of sugar in a 200 gram tub (and have an energy value of 200 calories), while other brands can be as low as 70 calories per tub.

Some shops advertise 'no fat, no sugar' cakes. Before you buy these, you should find out exactly what the product is made from. Often you will find such products contain honey, dried fruits or peanut butter which are high in calories.

Ingredients

Ingredients must be listed on products in the descending order of weight (quantity) that they occur in the product. The major ingredient is listed first, and the smallest ingredient is listed last. So if the first listed ingredient is sugar, then that means there is more sugar in the product than any other ingredient.

The shopping list

You may already have a number of these products in your cupboards, so always check to see what it is you need before writing up your shopping list.

Cereals

You can make up your own cereal mixture. This means that as well as having control over the ingredients, you can be sure that you will enjoy eating the result. Mixed cereal brands can be very expensive. You need to find a market that sells cereal items in bulk bins. You can purchase scoops of what you would like to include in your cereal, and then mix them together at home.

Bread

You should try and buy whole grain or fibre-enriched bread that has a calorie count of under 100 calories per slice. Raisin and cinnamon bread can also be on the shopping list provided they, too, have a count of 100 calories or less per slice, and each slice weighs 30-40 grams.

Find the nutritional breakdown on the back of the packet. Be aware that the manufacturers usually show the calorie count for two slices, so you would need to halve that count to get the value of one slice. For example: 'This packet contains 17 serves, 1 serve = 2 slices at 190 calories'. In this example each slice of bread has 95 calories.

Be careful that you are not tempted to buy fresh bread from bakeries without checking the calorie count of their products first. Some fresh breads have extremely high calorie counts per slice. There is also the danger that if the bread is not cut up, you will give yourself very generous slices which will contain more calories.

Crackers

As the calorie content of crackers varies between brands and biscuit types, this will mean that you could, for example, eat six crackers of a brand with a lower calorie count but only four if they have a higher calorie count. Remember to always check the box for the calorie count. One hundred calories of crackers is one carbohydrate serve.

The store cupboard

The following items are useful to have on hand. It is advisable to have a good selection of condiments in your kitchen so that you can season dishes without having to use tasty alternatives that are higher in fat. Following is a list of useful items.

100% fruit jam or diet jam
arborio rice (a true risotto rice)
artificial sweetener
beef stock powder
canola or olive oil cooking spray
chicken stock powder
chilli powder
corn thins
cranberry sauce
crepes (50 calories per crepe)
crushed garlic (look for a jar with no added oil)
curry powder (a Malaysian hot curry was used for all the recipes in this book)
diet jelly
light evaporated skim milk
low-fat dressings
mixed herbs
olive oil
prepared mustards (wholegrain, mild or hot)
red wine
salt and freshly ground black pepper
sweet chilli sauce
tinned fruit in natural juice
tinned pie fruits
white wine

Refrigerated and frozen products

These products can be high in fat, always buy low-fat varieties if they are available.

cheddar cheese
cottage cheese
feta cheese
filo pastry (fresh if available)
ice-cream
light sour cream
milk
oven fries (check calorie count and find one closest to 100 calories per 100g)
parmesan cheese, grated or block (to shave)
yoghurt, flavoured (must be under 50 calories per 100 grams)
yoghurt, plain unsweetened (most of the recipes use plain unsweetened low-fat yoghurt)

Cottage cheese may be frozen and then used when needed.

Light sour cream may be put into ice cube trays and frozen for use in cooking. The same procedure can be used with tomato paste.

To stop products such as jam, chutney and tomato paste from going mouldy, store them in the refrigerator upside down (on their lids). This looks funny but it works!

Kitchen utensils

You will need a variety of kitchen appliances and utensils. The following list can be used as a guide.

cooking dishes (for example, quiche dish, pie dish, individual pie dishes, ramekin dishes)
hand-held blender
kitchen food processor that blends and grates food (this will save time when preparing vegetables)
non-stick fry pan or wok
sharp knife
whisk

Healthy weight range (for men and women aged 18 years and over)

There are many reasons that the scales may not accurately reflect your weight loss. For example, if you are exercising and building muscle you may notice your body looks more toned, but because muscle weighs more than fat, your slimmer-looking body may not necessarily weigh less on the scales. It is a good idea to use the fit of your clothes as a guide to whether or not you are succeeding with your weight loss plan.

Note: It is unhealthy to drop below your minimum weight.

Height		Healthy body weight range	
Height (cm)	Feet and inches	Weight (kg)	Stones and pounds
142	4 8	40-50	6 4-7 12
145	4 9	42-52	6 8-8 3
147	4 10	44-55	6 13-8 9
150	4 11	45-56	7 1-8 12
152	5 0	46-58	7 4-9 2
155	5 1	48-60	7 8-9 7
157	5 2	50-62	7 12-9 11
160	5 3	51-64	8 0-10 1
163	5 4	53-66	8 5-10 6
165	5 5	55-68	8 9-10 10
168	5 6	56-71	8 11-11 3
170	5 7	58-72	9 2-11 5
173	5 8	60-75	9 6-11 12
175	5 9	62-77	9 11-12 2
178	5 10	63-79	9 13-12 7
180	5 11	65-81	10 4-12 11
183	6 0	68-85	10 10-13 6
185	6 1	69-86	10 13-13 8
188	6 2	71-88	11 3-13 13
190	6 3	72-90	11 7-14 4

This chart should be used as a guide only

My Success Graph

Week	Weight	Chest	Waist	Hips	Thigh
1					
2					
3					
4					
5					
6					
7					
8					
9					
10					
11					
12					
13					
14					
15					
16					
17					
18					
19					
20					

The importance of exercise

Exercise can help to relieve stress and elevate your mood. Your body burns off calories, reducing your fat levels and improving your shape by toning and strengthening your muscles. It improves circulation and may mean that you feel healthier and more energetic. It can also boost your immune system.

Doing regular exercise may help you to feel stronger and fitter and can help to prevent osteoporosis. It can give you a more positive attitude towards your body.

If you really want to lose body fat, you need to take aerobic (cardiovascular) exercise every day or, at least, every second day. A thirty-minute workout or three ten-minute sessions is recommended.

Suitable activities include walking, circuit training, swimming, water running, cycling or gym training.

Walking

Walking is one of the best types of aerobic exercise and is available to everyone. It is convenient and you can do it anywhere, anytime.

Make sure you purchase a good pair of walking shoes. Start off slowly and gently work yourself up to a good pace (you shouldn't be out of breath). Start with three thirty-minute sessions a week. (You could break these down into ten-minute segments until you build up your fitness level.) You will soon enjoy your walks. They provide a great opportunity to gather your thoughts or pop on a Walkman and listen to your favourite music.

Remember to protect your skin from the sun and drink plenty of water.

Resistance training

Resistance training can benefit you in many ways. It assists the maintenance of lean tissue and boosts fat loss (as well as burning up calories). Resistance training assists with the toning and shaping of your body, making you look and feel better. It helps improve your posture as well as strengthening both the abdominal and back muscles. It helps in the prevention of osteoporosis by strengthening your bones.

You do not need to attend a gym or buy expensive weight-lifting equipment to participate in this kind of exercise. A barbell with weights and dumbbells is sufficient.

Stretching

Flexibility is an important component of physical fitness. If you engage in regular stretching, you are likely to have improved flexibility. This may result in a decreased risk of injury and will help you to recover after exercising.

The basic principles of stretching are:

- warm up prior to stretching

- stretch before and after exercise

- stretch slowly and gently (take this time to relax and focus on your breathing)

- stretch to the point of gentle tension but never pain

- if something hurts, stop immediately - stretching should feel good, not painful.

You can make your stretching program last for as long or as short a time as you'd like. Start with a 5-10 minute program. As a guide each stretch should be held for at least 10 seconds. Repeat each stretch one to three times.

The following stretches represent basic exercises to complement a walking program. However, this is not a comprehensive guide. If you feel pain doing any of these stretches or are unsure as to exactly what it is you should be doing, you should seek professional advice from a doctor or physiotherapist. It is your responsibility to ensure you are performing the stretches correctly.

Calf stretch

Place one foot behind the other. Gently lean against a wall, with your back leg straight. You should feel a mild stretching sensation in the calf muscle of your back leg.

This stretch may be done with your back leg either straight or your back leg bent, so you feel the stretch lower in the calf.

Hamstring stretch

This stretch may be done in two different ways.

1 Sit on the floor with one leg extended out in front of you. Keeping the leg straight, gently bend forward at the hips until you feel a stretch in the back of the thigh (hamstring). Do not bend your back in order to get the chest closer to the knee; rather bend at the hips keeping your back straight.

2 Lie on your back. Grasp the back of one knee with both hands and gently pull the knee towards your chest. Holding your knee steady, gently straighten the lower leg until a stretch is felt in the back of the thigh.

Quadriceps stretch

In a standing position, gently pull the heel of one foot towards the buttock of that side until a stretch is felt at the front of the thigh.

Daily activity

Incidental exercise all adds up. For example just doing the housework can be wonderful exercise! You could also make choices in your regular activities that can increase your overall level of exercise. For example, take the stairs instead of the escalator or lift; park away from the supermarket and walk instead of driving around waiting for the closest park to the door. Walk to the shop to buy the newspaper instead of driving there. You should stop and think for a moment about where you can sneak some extra activities into your day.

Whatever exercise you choose to do, you're more likely keep it up if it's an activity that you enjoy. A mixture of aerobic and resistance exercise is highly recommended.

Commit yourself to an exercise regime now by setting yourself a goal. Remember to write it down and revise it regularly.

_____

_____

_____

_____

_____

_____

Average calories used in exercise

The benefits of exercise

Form of exercise	Rate of 'burn'	Examples of the exercise
Light exercise	4 calories per minute	slow walk, light cycling, social golf, canoeing, light gardening, housework, horse-riding, line dancing, ice skating
Moderate exercise	7 calories per minute	brisk walk, moderate cycling, easy swimming, light weight-training, racquet sports, basketball, light aqua-aerobics
Heavy exercise	10 calories per minute	power walking, jogging, vigorous cycling, strenuous swimming, heavy weight-training, skipping, boxing, advanced aqua-aerobics, strenuous dancing, climbing stairs, judo, cross country skiing

Note: You may choose an extra fruit or carbohydrate for each 30 minutes of aerobic exercise you do.

21-Day Plan

The next section will show you how easy it can be to put the Weigh Less Naturally food program together. There are twenty-one days of food plans to help you get started. You will see how you can have all the food units in one day while eating a variety of dishes using the recipes in this book. Remember that food is an important part of daily living, so you should enjoy what you eat. The recipes and planners are here to help you but there is nothing wrong with also cooking basic meals (such as steak, vegetables and mashed potato).

People have different food preferences, and not everybody is going to like every recipe. If you don't find the recipes used one day to your taste, you can just skip that day. However, it is recommended that you try the recipe first as you may be pleasantly surprised. One member of Weigh Less Naturally actually loved the Tuna and Celery Risotto (page 165) despite hating both tuna and celery!

Recipe serving sizes vary. It is easy to multiply or halve them to suit your family size.

You may repeat the days as often as you like. (This will have the added benefit of using up any leftovers.) Just be careful that you do not eat red meat or bacon more than four times each week. Have a variety of meat and make sure you choose days that also have chicken and fish. If you are following the plan strictly, but repeating and skipping days, that is fine. What you should not do is to mix up the meals from different days. Each day has been worked out according to the servings of the food units that you are supposed to have. If you substitute a meal from another day this may upset the balance of food groups. So while it is fine to substitute one day for another you should not substitute meals within the days on the plan.

The 21-day plan is based on the daily food allowances for women, so men and teenagers should add additional food servings to those listed. If you are cooking for a family and some members do not need to lose weight, make sure that they eat additional food.

Note: Some of your Optional Indulgences are already included in your Weigh Less Naturally day. They are incorporated into some of the recipes and are also utilised in foods such as ice cream. You will also have some Optional Indulgences left at the end of most days. These can be spent on your favourite treats. However, you need to check the calorie counts so you don't overeat or miscalculate. Remember that you may also save these up for weekends or special occasions – or just to have a bit of a splurge!

Why aren't the scales moving?

There is nothing worse than standing on your scales at the end of the week and finding out that you haven't lost any weight. If after being on the Weigh Less Naturally food program you are either not losing any weight or (even worse) still gaining weight, there is obviously a problem of some kind.

The important thing is not to let yourself feel defeated. There could be any number of things affecting your weight. Think about how your week really went. Has there been anything else in your life that could have affected you in this way? You should check each of the following things:

- your food diary
- whether you are correctly following the program
- your use of Optional Indulgences
- medications you are taking
- hormonal changes in your body

Food diary

Your food diary allows you to assess what you may have done wrong during that week. Check it carefully and add up all the food units to double check that you haven't accidentally over-eaten.

It can be very easy to snack absent-mindedly, without realising what you are doing. Are you picking and nibbling on leftovers, or suffering from 'diet amnesia'? Be sure to write down all snacking in your food diary so that you can accurately follow the program. Try to avoid nibbling and thinking that it doesn't matter. It does matter.

Following the Weigh Less Naturally food program

The program can be confusing to people initially. It's a good idea to check that you are following it correctly.

Make sure you clearly understand how many serves of each food group you are allowed. Do not mix up these groups. It is important that you do not change the program in any way. It will hamper your weight loss if you exchange, for example, one carbohydrate unit for a fruit unit. You need a balanced diet, and the program has been especially balanced for optimum weight loss.

You should also check that you are dividing the recipes up into the correct quantities. If the recipe serves four, you need to divide it up into four equal portions. A common error that parents with children can make is to serve the children first (usually with smaller serves) then eat half of the rest. This actually means you are having a bigger portion than you should be. It is very important to only have one serve of each dish.

Wrongly estimating your Optional Indulgences

Make sure that you calculate your Optional Indulgence calories very carefully. You need to take account of any that are used up in the recipes and have an accurate count of how you use up the rest.

For example, if you have a day where you eat one serve of Meringue Rice Pudding for breakfast, a Stuffed Pita Pocket for lunch and one serve of Pumpkin and Feta Filo Parcels for dinner and a Banana Smoothie for a snack, you need to remember that 10 Optional Indulgences were used for breakfast, 45 for dinner and 15 for the snack. So out of the 250 extra possible calories you started with, you only have 180 calories left. It is important to remember that a lot of the recipes use these Optional Indulgences – so you can't have a snack each day that uses up all 250 Optional Indulgence calories if any have been used in the recipes.

Another problem that can occur when using the Optional Indulgences is that you may not know the actual calorie count of the foods you are eating. Again, you really need a calorie counter with you so that you can check the exact figures. Sometimes foods that you do not think are very fatty can contain a surprisingly high calorie count. For example, some low-fat muffins sold in bakeries can have up to 400 calories in each muffin. Do not guess at the calorie count of foods. If they do not have a nutritional breakdown and are not listed in your calorie counter, it is better to avoid eating them!

Medications

If you have been sick, your body can retain fluids and give an inaccurate weight on the scales. Let your body get back to normal, wait until you feel better, and then see how you go.

Some medications can also affect your weight. Check with your doctor or pharmacist. Let your doctor know that you are trying to lose weight and talk about any issues that arise.

Hormonal changes

Your body can be affected by many things, including hormonal changes. These can cause you to retain fluids, which could be the reason you are not losing weight. Women, in particular, can be affected by this. If you know that you are likely to experience pre-menstrual bloating, don't worry about the slight weight gain that you will have during this period. Keep following the program and your weight loss should stay on track.

Binge eating

Some people are prone to binge eating. If you fall into this category, don't worry. You can stop it and take control of your eating habits. But first you must understand why it happens.

What things cause you to overeat? There are many causes of this problem including emotional triggers such as stress, loneliness, anger, and sadness as well as social triggers such as dining out with friends or having a good time at a party.

Read your food diary and try to recognise foods, emotions or situations that can lead to binge eating. As you become more aware of what is causing it, you can avoid those situations. For example, if you are more tempted to binge eat late in the afternoon because your energy levels are low, then change your diet so that you eat lots of small meals during the day – this will help the reduce the 'highs and lows' you might be feeling. Look for non-edible sources of comfort such as going for a walk, working in your flower garden or soaking in a warm bath.

If you feel that you are heading for a binge or if you catch yourself in the middle of one, you can still stop it. Simply walk away, leave everything where it is and get out of the situation that is causing the problem. A brisk walk around the block can give you time to think about what's making you want to eat. If you have bought a chocolate bar and eaten half of it, throw the rest away.

There may be times when you're nursing a craving that is so bad you have no choice about it. If you do, allow yourself to have a small serve of the food you desire. Really let yourself enjoy that serve, eat it slowly and relish it. But don't have any more.

If worst comes to worst and you indulge in an all-night 'binge eat', don't hate yourself afterwards. You have to accept what has happened and move on. Do not skip meals the next day as this could cause you to overeat again. You're far better off expending the energy by exercising. Try adding an extra half-hour to your next workout, and be very careful about what you eat over the next few days. It's also a good idea to go without your Optional Indulgences for that period.

Maintaining your weight loss

Once you have lost your weight the next question to ask is 'How do I keep it off?'

The answer is really quite simple. Remember that the Weigh Less Naturally food program is not a 'diet'. It is a lifestyle change that means you eat a healthy balanced diet with occasional indulgences and basic rules that you must follow in order to maintain your weight.

The six-week maintenance program

During the first six weeks on the maintenance program, you will need to add some more food to your weekly program. The way to do this is outlined below. Experiment with food. Add in small servings until you stop losing weight, and then strike a happy balance between eating more of the food you love and maintaining your weight. This balance will vary from person to person because everybody is unique with different lifestyles and metabolic rates. Your individual energy balance will depend on your age, the amount of exercise you do and your lifestyle.

Weigh yourself at the end of each week and record it. Evaluate this record. If you have lost weight, add a few more food units to the program for the next week. If you gain weight, repeat that same program for another week. If you again gain weight the next week, reduce the food units you added previously. Eventually you will get an indication of how much food you can take without gaining weight.

Once you have figured out your own maintenance program you need to follow it. Most people get through to week six and find that their weight has stabilised. If you happen to continue losing weight, add more food units until you stop.

You will find that your weight may vary from week to week. This will include natural weight fluctuations that occur because of such things as water retention and hormonal changes. You may find you develop a 'swing' in weight of 1-2 kilograms. That is fine and healthy, but if your weight continues to creep up over 2 kilograms, go straight back onto the Weigh Less Naturally program until you return to your ideal weight. A word of warning - don't leave it too long if you start to put on weight. Two kilograms can easily turn into four, and then into six if it is neglected. Then you will have a lot of hard work to do all over again!

With your maintenance program, you should be able to stay slim for the remainder of your life.

Six-week maintenance program

Week one

Add one carbohydrate or fruit unit to your program each day. Continue to fill out your food diary. Evaluate your weight. Did you lose weight, gain weight or stay the same? Use this information to plan your food for week two.

Week two

Add an extra 50 Optional Indulgence calories each day to your food program. Continue to fill out your food diary. Evaluate your weight. Did you lose weight, gain weight or stay the same?

Week three

Add one more carbohydrate, fruit or protein unit each day to the food program. Continue to fill out your food diary. Evaluate your weight. Did you lose weight, gain weight or stay the same?

Week four

Add another 50 Optional Indulgence calories each day to your food program. Continue to fill out your food diary. Evaluate your weight. Did you lose weight, gain weight or stay the same?

Week five

Continue to enjoy the extra units you have earned so far but do not add any more this week. Stop recording your food in your food diary, and try to keep track in your head. Evaluate your weight. Did you lose weight, gain weight or stay the same?

Week six

Continue to enjoy the extra units you have earned so far but do not add any more. However, you can relax a little more and treat yourself once during the week to a piece of cake, serve of ice cream or extra glass of wine without counting it. Continue to work out your food units in your head. Evaluate your weight. Did you lose weight, gain weight or stay the same?

After the maintenance program

Continue with the maintenance program as if you were still on week six. Maintaining your weight is much more relaxing than losing it. However, if you find yourself indulging a little too much and the scales start to creep up, go back to the Weigh Less Naturally food program for a week or two.

There are many reasons why some people may find that the weight starts to creep up.

Old bad habits slip back, such as nibbling, or eating too much high fat and sugar foods. These should be a luxury, not a part of your regular diet.

Some people stop cooking. It is important not to let lack of time force you into buying high-fat, take-away or convenience foods.

It can also be tempting to increase you food intake beyond what your body will maintain. This often happens when people who exercise stop exercising as much once they reach their desired goal, but continue to eat the same amount. If you reduce your exercise program for any reason, you must remember to cut off some of your extra food units and Optional Indulgence calories until you recommence your exercise routine.

If you have followed the maintenance program but you are still either losing weight after adding extra units to the maintenance program; or gaining weight after returning to the weight loss program, you should consult your doctor. There may be a medical reason behind your inability to maintain your weight.

The future

Believe that anything is possible. Stacey Hall would never have dreamt when she was 45 kilograms overweight that she would win a weight loss contest. I would never have dreamt that I would be helping thousands of people all around the world to do the same. So dream big, move forwards and have a happy prosperous life.

21-day plan

Day 1

Breakfast
30 g (1 oz) cereal
125 ml (4 fl oz) low-fat milk or 65 ml (2 fl oz) low-fat flavoured yoghurt
1 fruit serve (of your choice)

Lunch
Super Open Sandwich (page 156)

Dinner
Chicken Stroganoff (page 96)
½ cup cooked pasta
Steamed green vegetables
Meringue Rice Pudding (page 195)

Snacks
1 fruit serve (of your choice)

Water

Optional Indulgences used
Super Open Sandwich   45
Chicken Stroganoff   25
Meringue Rice Pudding   10
One extra dairy serve   40

Optional Indulgences spare
130

Day 2

Breakfast
Meringue Rice Pudding (page 195)
or
Breakfast from Day 1 (if you prefer this you will have 10 Optional Indulgences to spare!)

Lunch
Stuffed Pita Pocket (page 154)
1 fruit serve (of your choice)

Dinner
Pumpkin and Feta Filo Parcels (page 137)
Baked Vegetables (no potatoes) (page 77)
Steamed green vegetables

Snacks
Banana Smoothie (page 181)
4 corn thins and 1 tablespoon peanut butter

Water

Optional Indulgences used
Meringue Rice Pudding   10
Pumpkin and Feta Filo Parcels   20
Baked Vegetables   25
Banana Smoothie   15

Optional Indulgences spare
185

Day 3

Breakfast
30 g (1 oz) cereal
125 ml (4 fl oz) low-fat milk or 65 ml (2 fl oz) low-fat flavoured yoghurt
1 fruit serve (of your choice)

Lunch
Creamy Chicken Satay Salad (page 101)
1 fruit serve with diet jelly

Dinner
Spaghetti with Bolognaise Sauce (page 150)

Snacks
2 slices raisin or cinnamon toast with diet jam or 100% fruit jam
1 fruit serve (of your choice)

Water

Optional Indulgences used
Creamy Chicken Satay Salad   15
Spaghetti with Bolognaise Sauce   50

Optional Indulgences spare
185

Day 4

Breakfast

2 slices raisin or cinnamon toast with diet jam or 100% fruit jam
1 cup fresh fruit salad
200 ml (7 fl oz) diet yoghurt

Lunch

Ezy Bacon and Egg Pie (page 110)
Tossed green salad with low-fat dressing

Dinner

1 x 300 g (10 oz) potato baked in jacket
Creamy Chicken Satay Salad (page 101)

Snacks

Chocolate Banana Parcels (page 185)
Irish Cream Custard (page 193)
1 fruit serve (of your choice)

Water

Optional Indulgences used
Ezy Bacon and Egg Pie   20
Low-fat dressing   20
Cream Chicken Satay Salad   15
Chocolate Banana Parcel   100
Irish Cream Custard   40

Optional Indulgences spare
55

Day 5

Breakfast

30 g (1 oz) cereal

125 ml (4 fl oz) low-fat milk or 65 ml (2 fl oz) low-fat flavoured yoghurt

1 fruit serve (of your choice)

Lunch

2 slices bread

50 g (2 oz) chicken or turkey

1 tablespoon low-fat mayonnaise

Mixed salad (eg lettuce, tomato, cucumber)

Banana Smoothie (page 181)

Dinner

Tomato and Parmesan Risotto (page 163)

Tossed green salad with low-fat dressing

1 fruit serve with 100 ml low-fat icecream

Snacks

Cheesy Toast (page 86)

Water

Optional Indulgences used

Low-fat mayonnaise   20

Banana Smoothie   15

Tomato and Parmesan Risotto   10

Low-fat dressing   20

Low-fat icecream   70

Cheesy Toast Relish   20

Optional Indulgences spare

95

Day 6

Breakfast
30 g (1 oz) cereal
125 ml (4 fl oz) low-fat milk or 65 ml (2 fl oz) low-fat flavoured yoghurt
1 fruit serve (of your choice)

Lunch
B.L.E.T. (page 82)
Oven fries (pre-cooked oven fries from supermarket freezer. Check calorie
count and find one closest to 100 calories per 100g)

Dinner
Lemon Chicken and Cheese Pies (page 120)
Baked Vegetables (no potato in this) (page 77)
Steamed green vegetables
200 ml (7 oz) diet yoghurt
1 banana

Snacks
1 fruit serve of your choice

Water

Optional Indulgences used
B.L.E.T.   20
Oven fries   30
Lemon Chicken and Cheese Pies   40
Baked Vegetables   25

Optional Indulgences spare
135

This is a great weekend day.

Day 7

Brunch
Pancake Jack-a-Stack (page 198)
½ cup tinned peaches (or fruit of your choice)
125 ml (4 fl oz) low-fat yoghurt

Dinner
Beef Enchiladas (page 80)
Tossed green salad with low-fat dressing

Snacks
1 fruit serve with diet jelly
1 serve crackers and 2 slices of low-fat cheese

Water

Optional Indulgences used
Beef Enchiladas   20

Optional Indulgences spare
230

This is a great weekend day.

Day 8

Breakfast

30 g (1 oz) cereal
125 ml (4 fl oz) low-fat milk or 65 ml (2 fl oz) low-fat flavoured yoghurt
1 fruit serve (of your choice)

Lunch

Turkey and Cranberry Sub (page 168)

Dinner

Salmon Quiche (page 143)
Tossed green salad with low-fat dressing
1 fruit serve and 200 ml low-fat yoghurt

Snacks

Devonshire tea (Berry Nice Scones page 182)
1 fruit serve (of your choice)

Water

Optional Indulgences used
Turkey and Cranberry Sub   20
Low-fat dressing   20
Devonshire tea and cream   35

Optional Indulgences spare
180

Day 9

Breakfast
30 g (1 oz) cereal
125 ml (4 fl oz) low-fat milk or 65 ml (2 fl oz) low-fat flavoured yoghurt
1 fruit serve (of your choice)

Lunch
Salmon Quiche (page 143)
Tossed green salad and low-fat dressing

Dinner
Chop Suey in a Jiffy (page 97)
1 serve carbohydrate (eg rice, potato or more noodles)
1 Fruit Turnover (page 190)
100 ml (4 fl oz) low-fat icecream

Snacks
Devonshire tea (Berry Nice Scones page 182)
diet jelly with 200 ml low-fat yoghurt

Water

Optional Indulgences used
Low-fat dressing   20
Chop Suey in a Jiffy   25
Fruit Turnover   30
Low-fat icecream   70

Optional Indulgences spare
105

Day 10

Breakfast
2 slices raisin or cinnamon toast with diet jam
1 banana

Lunch
Super Open Sandwich (page 156)

Dinner
Vegetarian Lasagne (page 173)
Tossed green salad with low-fat dressing
Baked Apricot Cheesecake (page 179)

Snacks
1 fruit serve (of your choice)

Water

Optional Indulgences used
Super Open Sandwich   45
Vegetarian Lasagne   25
Low-fat dressing   20
Baked Apricot Cheesecake   35

Optional Indulgences spare
125

Day 11

Breakfast

30 g (1 oz) cereal
125 ml (4 fl oz) low-fat milk or 65 ml (2 fl oz) low-fat flavoured yoghurt
1 fruit serve (of your choice)

Lunch

Ham and Cheese Pie (page 114)
Tossed green salad with low-fat dressing

Dinner

Chicken Noodle Stir-fry (page 93)

Snacks

Chocolate Mousse (page 186)
1 fruit serve (of your choice)
1 carbohydrate serve (of your choice)

Water

Optional Indulgences used
Ham and Cheese Pie   55
Low-fat dressing   20
Chicken Noodle Stir-fry   20
Chocolate Mousse   40

Optional Indulgences spare
115

Day 12

Breakfast
Banana Smoothie (page 181)
1 cup fresh fruit salad

Lunch
1 serve French Onion Cheeseball (page 68)
2 serves of crackers of choice (you could add carrot sticks or celery sticks)

Dinner
Pasta Carbonara (page 127)
Tossed green salad with low-fat dressing

Snacks
Cheesy Toast (page 86)
1 fruit serve (of your choice)

Water

Optional Indulgences used
Banana Smoothie   15
French Onion Cheeseball   40
Pasta Carbonara   10
Low-fat dressing   20
Cheesy Toast   45

Optional Indulgences spare
140

Day 13

Breakfast

30 g (1 oz) cereal
125 ml (4 fl oz) low-fat milk or 65 ml (2 fl oz) low-fat flavoured yoghurt
1 fruit serve (of your choice)

Lunch

Tomato and Parmesan Risotto (page 163)
1 fruit serve
200 ml (7 oz) low-fat yoghurt

Dinner

Tacos (page 159)
Tossed green salad with low-fat dressing

Snacks

Vanilla Slice (page 205)
1 fruit serve (of your choice)

Water

Optional Indulgences used
Tomato and Parmesan Risotto   10
Tacos   20
Low-fat dressing   20
Vanilla Slice   80

Optional Indulgences spare
120

Day 14

Breakfast
1 rasher bacon, grilled
1 egg, dry fried or poached
1 slice toast with diet jam
1 fruit serve (of your choice)

Lunch
Savoury Fritters (page 145)
Tossed green salad with low-fat dressing

Dinner
Wholegrain Vegetable Parcel (page 175)
Baked Vegetables (no potato in this) (page 77)
Steamed green vegetables
Jelly Whip (page 194)
1 cup of fresh fruit salad

Snacks
Vanilla Slice (page 205)
1 fruit serve (of your choice)

Water

Optional Indulgences used
Low-fat dressing   20
Wholegrain Vegetable Parcel   10
Baked Vegetables   25
Vanilla Slice   80

Optional Indulgences spare
115

Day 15

Breakfast
30 g (1 oz) cereal
125 ml (4 fl oz) low-fat milk or 65 ml (2 fl oz) low-fat flavoured yoghurt
1 fruit serve (of your choice)

Lunch
Soy and Honey Warm Chicken Caesar Salad (page 149)
Crusty bread roll

Dinner
Pumpkin and Bean Risotto (page 136)
1 cup fresh fruit salad
200 ml (7 oz) diet yoghurt

Snacks
1 serve crackers with 1 slice cheese and tomato
1 fruit serve (of your choice)

Water

Optional indulgences used
Soy and Honey Warm Chicken Caesar Salad   20
Pumpkin and Bean Risotto   20

Optional Indulgences spare
210

Day 16

Breakfast
Cheesy Toast (page 86)

Lunch
Peachy Pancakes (page 200)
3 teaspoons maple syrup (this uses up 45 Optional Indulgences)

> Try heating the syrup in the microwave – this thins it down and makes it go further!

Dinner
Stuffed Crispy Chicken with Chutney Sauce (page 153)
Steamed green vegetables
150 g (5 oz) baked potato

Snacks
diet jelly
1 fruit serve (of your choice)
100 ml (4 fl oz) low-fat icecream

Water

Optional Indulgences used
Cheesy Toast   45
Stuffed Crispy Chicken   10
Low-fat icecream   70

Optional Indulgences spare
125

Day 17

Breakfast

30 g (1 oz) cereal
125 ml (4 fl oz) low-fat milk 65 ml (2 fl oz) low-fat flavoured yoghurt
1 fruit serve (of your choice)

Lunch

Super Open Sandwich (page 156)

Dinner

Rich Beef Stroganoff (page 139)
1 serve fruit with diet jelly

Snacks

Banana and Blueberry Muffin (page 180)
1 fruit serve (of your choice)
200 ml diet yoghurt

Water

Optional Indulgences used
Super Open Sandwich   45
Rich Beef Stroganoff   35
Banana and Blueberry Muffin   30

Optional Indulgences spare
140

Day 18

Breakfast

Banana and Blueberry Muffin (warmed) (page 180)
1 cup fresh fruit salad
200 ml (7 oz) low-fat yoghurt

Lunch

Creamy Chicken Satay Salad (page 101) served on shredded lettuce
1 fruit serve (of your choice)

Dinner

Perfect Pizza (page 130)
Oven fries (check calorie count and find one closest to
100 calories per 100g)

Snacks

1 slice raisin or cinnamon toast with diet jam
1 fruit serve (of your choice)

Water

Optional Indulgences used
Banana and Blueberry Muffin   30
Creamy Chicken Satay Salad   15
Oven Fries   30

Optional Indulgences spare
175

Day 19

Breakfast
½ cup baked beans
1 tomato, halved and grilled
1 cup mushrooms, sliced and sauteed
1 slice toast

Lunch
Chicken, Cheese and Pineapple Monster Salad Roll (page 88)
1 fruit serve (of your choice)

Dinner
Macaroni Magic (page 122)
Tossed green salad with low-fat dressing

Snacks
1 fruit serve (of your choice)

Water

Optional Indulgences used
Chicken, Cheese and Pineapple Monster Salad Roll   20
Macaroni Magic   10
Low-fat dressing   20

Optional Indulgences spare
200

Day 20

Breakfast
30 g (1 oz) cereal
125 ml (4 fl oz) low-fat milk or 65 ml (2 fl oz) low-fat flavoured yoghurt
1 fruit serve (of your choice)

Lunch
5-Minute Singapore Noodles (page 111)
1 fruit serve (of your choice)

Dinner
Chicken Chilli Parcels (page 89)
Baked Vegetables (no potato in this) (page 77)
Green steamed vegetables

Snacks
1 serve Orange and Mango Cheesecake (page 197)
1 fruit serve (of your choice)

Water

Optional Indulgences used
5-Minute Singapore Noodles   20
Chicken Chilli Parcels   45
Baked Vegetables   25
Orange and Mango Cheesecake   20

Optional Indulgences spare
150

Day 21

Breakfast
1 raisin or cinnamon toast with diet jam
1 cup fresh fruit salad
200 ml (7 oz) low-fat yoghurt

Lunch
B.L.E.T. (page 82)
Oven fries (check calorie count and find one closest to
100 calories per 100 g)

Dinner
Pork and Cashew Stir-fry (page 131)
Chocolate Mousse (page 186)

Snacks
1 fruit serve (of your choice)

Water

Optional Indulgences used
B.L.E.T.   20
Oven fries   30
Pork and Cashew Stir-fry   20
Chocolate Mousse   40

Optional Indulgences spare
140

The Weigh Less Naturally Program Recipes

Soups and Dips

Cream of Broccoli Soup

A lovely warming soup, this is great to have with crusty bread.

Serves 4
1 large onion, diced
300 g (10 oz) potato, peeled, diced small
1 teaspoon butter
500 g (16 oz) broccoli, chopped
3¼ cups (26 fl oz) water
2 teaspoons chicken stock powder
1 teaspoon garam masala
1 cup (8 fl oz) low-fat milk
1 tablespoon light sour cream

1   Melt the butter in a pan and lightly sauté the onion and potato for a few minutes.

2   Add the remaining ingredients except for the milk and sour cream. Bring to the boil and simmer for 20 minutes or until the vegetables are soft.

3   Remove from the heat and cool slightly. Blend.

4   Stir in the milk and reheat. Add the sour cream and swirl through the soup. Serve.

Food units per serve
½ D = milk
½ CB = potato
20 Optional Indulgences = butter, sour cream

Creamy Prawn and Sweetcorn Soup

Serves 4

1 litre (36 fl oz) water
2 teaspoons chicken stock powder
150 g (5 oz) prawns or 130 g (4½ oz) of any other seafood
440 g (16 oz) creamed corn
1 teaspoon soy sauce
salt and freshly ground black pepper to taste
2 tablespoons cornflour
2 egg whites
4 spring onions, finely diced

This makes a large bowl and is very filling. If you don't eat seafood, you can substitute 100 g chicken.

---

1 Bring the water and stock powder to the boil in a pan.

2 Add the seafood, creamed corn, soy sauce, salt and pepper. Bring to the boil, then simmer for 5 minutes.

3 Mix the cornflour with a little water and add to the soup, stirring slowly. Stir until thickened.

4 Lightly whisk the egg whites. Remove the soup from the heat and stir through the egg whites and spring onions. Serve immediately.

Food units per serve
½ PR = seafood
1½ CB = corn
20 Optional Indulgences = cornflour, egg whites

Curry Tomato Soup

A lovely and warm soup, this is great to have with crusty bread.

Serves 2
1 teaspoon butter
1 large onion, diced
1 teaspoon curry powder
410 g (14 oz) tinned diced tomatoes
1 clove garlic, diced or minced
2 cups carrots, diced
1 cup celery, diced
1 teaspoon beef or chicken stock powder
500 ml (16 fl oz) water
handful of fresh herbs (such as basil, parsley, tarragon, thyme)
1 tablespoon light sour cream

1   Melt the butter in a pan and lightly sauté the onion and curry powder for a few minutes.

2   Add the remaining ingredients except for the sour cream. Bring to the boil and simmer for 20 minutes or until the vegetables are soft.

3   Remove from the heat and cool slightly. Blend. Add the sour cream and swirl it through the soup. Serve.

Food units per serve
30 Optional Indulgences = butter, sour cream

French Onion Cheese Ball

This dish is excellent at a party

or a lunch.

Serves 4
1 cup smooth cottage cheese
100 g (4 oz) low-fat cheese, grated
2 tablespoons light sour cream
1 packet French onion soup mix
3 sticks celery, finely diced
1 small red onion, finely diced
poppy seeds

1   Mix all the ingredients together except the poppy seeds.

2   Sprinkle the poppy seeds onto a tray or baking dish.

3   Place the mixture on top and gently shape it into a ball. The mix may be sticky but it will firm up in the refrigerator. Roll the ball in poppy seeds.

4   Leave the ball in the refrigerator for a minimum of 1 hour. Serve with crackers or Lavish Bread Crisps (page 119).

Food units per serve
2 PR or 1 PR and 2 D = cheeses
40 Optional Indulgences = sour cream, soup mix

Fruit Cheese Log

Serves 4
1 cup smooth cottage cheese
100 g (4 oz) low-fat cheese, grated
2 tablespoons light sour cream
60 g (2 oz) mixed dried fruit
4 tablespoons poppy seeds

1 Mix all the ingredients together except the poppy seeds.

2 Sprinkle the poppy seeds onto a tray or onto baking paper.

3 Shape the mixture into a log shape and roll to coat in poppy seeds.

4 Place on a serving tray and cover with plastic wrap. Refrigerate until ready to serve.

This can be served with rice crackers (12 crackers = 1 CB). This dish is excellent at a party or a lunch.

Food units per serve
2 PR or 1 Pr and 2 D = cheese
$\frac{1}{2}$ F = dried fruit
20 Optional Indulgences = sour cream

Golden Pumpkin Soup

This is a lovely soup to have with crusty bread, fritters or pancakes

Serves 4
1 teaspoon butter
1 large onion, diced
300 g (10 oz) sweet potato, peeled and diced
1 clove garlic, minced
2 stalks celery, diced
1 teaspoon curry paste
400 g (14 oz) pumpkin, peeled and diced
1 teaspoon stock powder, beef or chicken
1 litre (35 fl oz) water
1 bay leaf
salt and freshly ground black pepper to taste
125 ml (4 fl oz) low-fat milk or buttermilk
parsley to garnish

1 Melt the butter in a pan and lightly sauté the onion, sweet potato, garlic, celery and curry paste until the potato is soft.

2 Add the remaining ingredients except for the milk and parsley. Bring to the boil and simmer for 20 minutes or until the vegetables are soft.

3 Remove from the heat and cool slightly. Remove the bay leaf and discard.

4 Add the milk slowly and blend. Garnish with parsley and serve.

Food units per serve
½ CB = potato
25 Optional Indulgences = butter, milk

Roast Pumpkin Dip

Serves 2
400 g (14 oz) pumpkin
2 teaspoons taco seasoning
2 cloves garlic, minced
juice of 1/2 lemon
salt to taste
Lavish Bread Chips (page 119)

1 Preheat the oven to 200°C.

2 Wash and de-seed the pumpkin and dry roast in the oven (skin on) until soft.

3 Peel the pumpkin and mash. Add the other ingredients. Chill.

4 Serve on Lavish Bread Chips (page 119).

> **Please note that most low-fat commercial dips cost you 20 optional units per teaspoon!**

Food units per serve
Roast Pumpkin Dip is free. There are no food units except those from the Lavish Bread Chips.

Sue's Minestrone

Serves 4

1 teaspoon olive oil
100 g (4 oz) ham, chopped
3 sticks celery, sliced
2 carrots, sliced
1 clove garlic, minced
1 tablespoon fresh parsley, chopped
½ cup macaroni, uncooked
2 teaspoons beef stock powder
1 litre (35 fl oz) water
410 g (14 oz) tinned crushed tomatoes
410 g (14 oz) tinned four bean mix
salt and freshly ground black pepper to taste

1   Heat the oil in a pot. Add the ham, celery, carrots and garlic and sauté for approximately 3 minutes.

2   Add all the other ingredients (except the beans mix) and stir well. Simmer for 30 minutes.

3   Add the four bean mix and simmer for a further 10-15 minutes. Add salt and pepper to taste and serve.

Food units per serve
2 PR = beans, ham
35 Optional Indulgences = oil
½ CB = noodles

Tomato Dip

Serves 6
1 cup smooth cottage cheese
1 tablespoon light sour cream
1 tablespoon low-fat mayonnaise
2 tablespoons tomato sauce
1 large tomato, skinned, finely chopped
2 spring onions, finely chopped
chilli powder to taste
freshly ground black pepper to taste

1 Blend together the cottage cheese, sour cream, mayonnaise and tomato sauce.

2 Stir through the tomato, spring onion, chilli and pepper.

3 Chill and serve.

> This dip can be served with carrot or celery sticks, rice crackers, corn thins, Savoury Fritters (page 145) or Lavish Bread Chips (page 119).
>
> To skin a tomato, plunge it into boiling water for 30 seconds, remove, pierce the skin and peel.

Food units per serve
1 D = cottage cheese
20 Optional Indulgences = sour cream, mayonnaise, tomato sauce

Lunches and Dinners

Asparagus and Walnut Pie

Serves 4

2 cups cooked brown rice
1 egg
2 tablespoons parmesan cheese, grated
4 tablespoons walnuts, chopped
50 g (2 oz) low-fat feta cheese
400 g (14 oz) tinned asparagus
2 eggs
125 ml (4 fl oz) low-fat milk
125 ml (4 fl oz) low-fat unsweetened yoghurt
2 cloves garlic, minced
1 tomato, sliced
salt and freshly ground black pepper to taste

1   Combine the cold cooked rice with the egg and parmesan cheese. Spread over the base of a pie dish sprayed with cooking spray. Bake at 180ºC for approximately 15 minutes or until the egg is set.

2   Sprinkle walnuts over the rice base, place the asparagus over the walnuts and crumble the feta cheese on top of the asparagus.

3   Blend together the eggs, milk, yoghurt, garlic and seasoning. Pour over the asparagus and place sliced tomato on top. Bake in the oven at 180ºC for 25 minutes or until the pie is set and lightly browned.

> This pie is delicious hot or cold and slices beautifully. If you choose to freeze it, reheat it and serve it hot. Broccoli may be used instead of asparagus.

Food units per serve
1 PR = egg, nuts, cheese
1 CB = rice
³/₄ D = milk, yoghurt

Baked Vegetables

Serves 1
vegetables of your choice
olive oil
lemon juice or balsamic vinegar
seasoning

1 Choose which vegetables you would like. Pumpkin, parsnip, carrot or choko are good choices, as they are 'free' vegetables. (Potato can be added but you will need to count this as a carbohydrate unit.)

2 Place ½ teaspoon of olive oil into a plastic bag with a splash of lemon juice or vinegar. Add the seasoning.

3 Cut the vegetables into bite-size pieces and add to the bag. Seal the bag and roll the vegetables until they are coated.

4 Remove from the bag and place on a greased tray. Bake at 200°C until cooked.

You can make this recipe to serve as many people as you want. Just remember to adjust the amount of oil and spices used with the amount of vegetables.

If you are in a hurry place the bag of vegetables in microwave for 5-10 minutes and then finish off in the oven. Remember to prick the bag before microwaving or it may explode!

Experiment by adding different herbs before cooking.

Food units per serve
25 Optional Indulgences = oil

Beef and Mushroom Crepes

Serves 4
300 g (10 oz) lean beef or lamb mince
1 large onion, diced
½ red capsicum, diced
½ green capsicum, diced
2 cloves garlic, minced
125 ml (4 fl oz) red wine
2 teaspoons sweet paprika powder
1 tablespoon sweet chilli sauce
1 teaspoon beef stock powder
1 tablespoon cornflour
2 tablespoons light sour cream
300 g (10 oz) mushrooms, sliced
8 crepes
410 g (14 oz) tinned crushed tomatoes
50 g (2 oz) low-fat cheese, grated
salt and freshly ground black pepper to taste

1 Sauté the mince with the onion, capsicum and garlic. Add the wine and cook until the vegetables are tender.

2 Season with stock powder, salt and pepper, paprika and chilli sauce. Add the mushrooms and cook for 3 minutes. Mix the cornflour with the sour cream and stir into mix. Cool.

3 Take one crepe and immerse it briefly in warm water. Shake the excess water off and lay it flat on the bench. Place an eighth of the mixture at one end of the crepe, roll up and place in an oven-proof dish. Repeat until all 8 crepes are filled.

4 Spread the tomatoes over the crepes and sprinkle with cheese. Bake the crepes at 180°C for 20-25 minutes. Serve with steamed green vegetables.

Look for crepes that have a calorie count of around 50 calories per crepe. You should also check the manufacturer's instructions for use. Some may not need to be immersed in water.

Food units per serve
1 CB = crepes
2 PR = mince, cheese
20 Optional Indulgences = sour cream, cornflour

Beef Enchiladas

Serves 2
150 g (5 oz) lean beef mince
1 onion, finely diced
1 clove garlic, minced
chilli powder to taste
1 cup mushrooms, diced
125 g (4 oz) frozen spinach, thawed and well drained
water
4 enchilada tortillas
50 g (2 oz) low-fat cheese, grated

Tomato sauce
water
1 small onion, diced
1 teaspoon taco seasoning
400 g (14 oz) tinned diced tomatoes

Topping
¼ cup (2 fl oz) low-fat unsweetened yoghurt
1 tablespoon light sour cream
2 spring onions, finely chopped

1 Pre-heat the oven to 200°C.

2 Sauté the beef, onion and garlic in a non-stick pan until browned. Add chilli powder, mushrooms and spinach and cook for 5 minutes.

3 To make the tomato sauce, heat a pan, add a little water and cook the onion until soft. Add the taco seasoning and tomatoes and simmer for about 10 minutes or until the sauce has thickened.

4 To make the enchiladas soften the tortillas according to the instructions on the packet (you could put them in the microwave for 40 seconds on high). Divide the beef mixture among the four tortillas. Roll up and place in an oven-proof dish and pour over the tomato sauce. Sprinkle the cheese over the top and bake in the oven at 200°C for 30-35 minutes.

5 To make topping, mix together the yoghurt and sour cream and serve over the enchiladas. Garnish with the spring onions.

Food units per serve
2 PR = mince, cheese
1 D = yoghurt, cheese
2 CB = tortillas
20 Optional Indulgences = sour cream

B.L.E.T.

This is a wonderful weekend treat.

Serves 1
2 slices wholegrain bread
1 rasher lean bacon
1 egg
2 teaspoons low-fat mayonnaise
2 teaspoons fruit chutney
1 large tomato, thickly sliced
lettuce, shredded

1   Grill the bacon until crispy. Dry fry the egg in a non-stick pan, turning it over to cook through. Toast the bread.

2   Mix the mayonnaise and chutney and spread over the toast. Layer the bacon, egg, tomato and lettuce. Place the second piece of toast on top to make a sandwich. Slice in half and serve with tossed green salad.

> If you have carbohydrate to spare you could have fries. Buy oven bake fries but check the calorie count. 100 g is usually close to 100 calories.

Food units per serve
2 PR = bacon, egg
2 CB = bread
20 Optional Indulgences = chutney, mayonnaise

Broccoli Fettuccine with Cream Sauce

Serves 4
1 large onion, halved and sliced
3 cloves garlic, minced
1 teaspoon butter
375 ml (12 fl oz) light evaporated milk
1 tablespoon cornflour
1 teaspoon prepared mustard
1 tablespoon light sour cream
50 g (2 oz) mozzarella cheese
salt and freshly ground black pepper to taste
4 cups cooked fresh fettuccine
700 g (25 oz) broccoli florets, steamed
4 tablespoons parmesan cheese, shaved

1   Sauté the onions and garlic in butter until tender.

2   Blend together the evaporated milk, cornflour and mustard. Pour over the onions and bring to the boil slowly, stirring constantly until thickened. Add the sour cream, mozzarella cheese and seasonings and stir through.

3   Drain the fettuccine and broccoli and place in a bowl. Pour the cream sauce over the fettuccine and broccoli. Sprinkle with parmesan cheese and serve immediately.

> To prevent broccoli going a grey colour once steamed, run under cold water for a brief second. This keeps it bright green.

Food units per serve
1 PR = cheese
2 CB = fettuccine
1½ D = milk
20 Optional Indulgences = cornflour, butter

Broccoli Macaroni Cheese

Serves 2
1 large head of broccoli
1 clove of garlic, minced
100 g (4 oz) low-fat cheese, grated
65 ml (2 fl oz) low-fat unsweetened yoghurt
2 teaspoons prepared mild mustard
1 teaspoon cornflour
125 g (4½ oz) pineapple, crushed
salt and freshly ground black pepper to taste
2 cups cooked macaroni pasta

1 Steam or microwave the broccoli until it is barely cooked. Drain and run under cold water to keep it a nice bright green colour.

2 Mix together the remaining ingredients in a bowl.

3 Toss the broccoli through the mixture.

4 Place in a baking dish and bake at 180°C for 20-25 minutes.

Food units per serve
2 PR = cheese
2 CB = pasta
½ F = pineapple
½ D = yoghurt
10 Optional Indulgences = cornflour

Caramelised Pumpkin and Onion Bake

This is a wonderful side dish to a meal and uses only a small number of food units.

Serves 4
750 g (28 oz) pumpkin, peeled and cut into large chunks (sweet pumpkin such as jap or butternut works best)
8 small onions, cut into quarters
8 cloves garlic, peeled and whole
4 teaspoons butter, melted
4 teaspoons brown sugar
2 teaspoons cornflour
3 tablespoons water

1 Pre-heat the oven to 200°C.

2 Place the pumpkin, onions and garlic in an oven-proof dish.

3 Mix together the butter, sugar, cornflour and water and pour over the vegetables.

4 Bake in the oven at 200°C for 40 minutes or until the pumpkin is soft and brown on the outside.

Food units per serve
55 Optional Indulgences = butter, sugar, cornflour

Cheesy Toast

Serves 1
1 slice bread
1 tablespoon relish
25 g (1 oz) grated cheese or low-fat cheese slice

1 Spread bread with relish.

2 Sprinkle cheese on top and grill until cheese bubbles. Serve.

Food units per serve
1 CB = bread
1 D = cheese
20 Optional Indulgences = relish

Chicken and Pineapple Stir-fry

Serves 4

400 g (14 oz) chicken
2 tablespoons soy sauce
1 teaspoon olive oil
1 large onion, cut into wedges
300 g (10 oz) carrots, cut into matchsticks
1 red capsicum, diced
4 large sticks celery, finely diced
250 g (8 oz) pineapple pieces (in natural juice)
500 g (16 oz) Chinese cabbage, shredded
1 cup snow peas or bean sprouts
1 tablespoon cornflour
2 teaspoons chicken stock powder
125 ml (4 fl oz) water
2 cups cooked rice

1 Sauté the chicken and soy sauce in the oil until cooked, remove from the pan and set aside.

2 Add the onion, carrot, capsicum and celery to the pan and stir-fry until tender.

3 Return the chicken to the pan with the pineapple, cabbage and snow peas. Heat through but take care not to overcook the cabbage.

4 Mix together the cornflour, chicken stock and water. Pour into the pan and heat until thickened, stirring constantly. Serve on rice.

Food units per serve
2 PR = chicken
1 CB = rice
½ F = pineapple
20 Optional Indulgences = cornflour

Chicken, Cheese and Pineapple Monster Salad Roll

Serves 1
1 x 50 g (2 oz) large bread roll
50 g (2 oz) cold chicken
1 slice of cheese
1 slice of pineapple
2 teaspoons low-fat mayonnaise
lettuce, chopped
tomato, sliced
cucumber, sliced
sprouts

1 Cut bread roll in half lengthways. Spread mayonnaise in the middle.

2 Add all other ingredients to taste. Serve.

Food units per serve
2 CB = bread
1 PR = chicken
1 D = cheese
½ F = pineapple
20 Optional Indulgences = mayonnaise

Chicken Chilli Parcels

Serves 2

8 sun-dried or dehydrated tomatoes
100 g (4 oz) chicken, diced small
1 teaspoon olive oil
250 g (8 oz) mushrooms, finely diced
1 red capsicum, diced
1 large onion, diced
125 ml (4 fl oz) low-fat unsweetened yoghurt
1 tablespoon cornflour
1 tablespoon sweet chilli sauce
salt and freshly ground black pepper to taste
6 sheets filo pastry
1 egg white, beaten lightly
sesame seeds to garnish

1   Soak the tomatoes in a little boiling water for 5 minutes to reconstitute, then dice.

2   Sauté the chicken in the oil, then remove and set aside.

3   Add the mushrooms, capsicum and onion to the pan and saute until almost cooked. Add the dried tomatoes and cooked chicken and cool.

4   Mix together the yoghurt, cornflour, chilli sauce, salt and pepper. Add to the mushroom mix.

5   Take one sheet of filo and fold it into three. Place a sixth of the filling at one end of the filo, roll filo over once, tuck in the sides and roll to the end. Pastry brush the filo parcel with the egg white and sprinkle with sesame seeds. Repeat this procedure until you have 6 parcels. (You can make 2 large parcels using 3 sheets of layered filo if you prefer.) Bake at 180ºC for 25 minutes. Serve with salad or baked vegetables.

Freeze the parcels when cooked and reheat in the oven to crisp up. They make great finger food.

Fresh filo is best. You will usually find it in the supermarket near the fresh noodles in the refrigerator section. It keeps for 3-5 weeks in the refrigerator.

Food units per serve
1 PR = chicken
1 CB = filo
1 D = yoghurt
45 Optional Indulgences = cornflour, egg white, oil

Chicken Lasagne

Serves 4
4 cups pumpkin, diced
2 large sticks celery, finely diced
1 large onion, diced
2 teaspoons chicken stock powder
300 g (10 oz) potato, diced
1 teaspoon olive oil
350 g (12 oz) chicken mince
1 teaspoon oregano, dried
210 g (7 oz) lasagne sheets (instant pre-cooked)
250 g (8 oz) frozen spinach, thawed and well drained

Topping
250 ml (8 fl oz) low-fat unsweetened yoghurt
1 egg
125 ml (4 fl oz) low-fat milk
1 teaspoon prepared mustard
50 g (2 oz) low-fat cheddar cheese

1 Place the pumpkin, celery, onion and stock in a pot, cover with water and cook. Drain and cool.

2 Cook the potato and mash when tender.

3 Sauté the chicken and oregano in the oil. Cool.

4 Line a large oven-proof dish with a layer of lasagne sheets, place a layer of chicken, then pumpkin mix, then spinach, then lasagne and repeat layering until the final layer, spread over mashed potato.

5 Mix together the topping ingredients and pour them over the potato. Bake at 180ºC for approximately 45 minutes. Serve hot or cold with salad.

You may like to substitute the chicken with minced beef, tuna or salmon.

Food units per serve
2 PR = chicken mince, egg
2 CB = lasagne
2 D = yoghurt, cheese
25 Optional Indulgences = milk, oil

Chicken Noodle Stir-fry

Serves 4
185 g (6 oz) hokkien noodles (approximately 2 cups)
1 teaspoon olive oil
400 g (14 oz) chicken, diced or in strips
1 large onion, sliced
2 cloves garlic, minced
2 teaspoons fresh ginger, grated
1 red capsicum, thinly sliced
2 small carrots, thinly sliced
250 g (8 oz) cabbage, shredded
200 g (7 oz) snow peas
2 tablespoons soy sauce
2 tablespoons black bean sauce
1 teaspoon chicken stock powder
1 tablespoon cornflour
125 ml (4 fl oz) water

1   Place the noodles in a fine sieve, rinse under warm water, and drain well.

2   Heat the oil in a wok or large pan, add the chicken and stir-fry until cooked. Remove from the pan and set aside.

3   Add the onion, garlic, ginger, capsicum and carrot to the pan and stir-fry until just tender. Add the cabbage and snow peas and cook for 2 minutes. Return chicken to the pan with the noodles.

4   Combine the soy and black bean sauce with the chicken stock, cornflour and water. Add to the stir-fry and cook until the sauce boils and thickens.

Food units per serve
2 PR = chicken
1 CB = noodles
20 Optional Indulgences = cornflour, oil

Chicken Pop-overs

These little pop-overs are wonderful the next day.

Serves 4
350 g (11 oz) chicken mince
1 onion, finely diced
1 large carrot, grated
1 cup pumpkin, grated
1 tablespoon flour
1 teaspoon dried rosemary
1 tablespoon soy sauce
salt and freshly ground black pepper to taste

Batter
1 cup self-raising flour
250 ml (8 fl oz) low-fat milk
1 egg
salt and freshly ground black pepper to taste

1   Pre-heat the oven to 200°C.

2   In a bowl, mix together the chicken, onion, carrot, pumpkin, flour, rosemary, soy sauce and salt and pepper. (Using your hand to mix is the easiest and quickest way.)

3   Lightly spray a muffin tin (12 muffins) with cooking spray. Divide the meat mixture evenly between the muffin moulds. Place in the oven and cook for 10 minutes.

4   Mix the batter ingredients together with a whisk.

5 Remove the muffin tin from the oven and spoon the batter evenly over each muffin. Return to the oven and cook for approximately 20 minutes until the batter is browned and puffy. Remove and serve with baked vegetables and peas or salad.

Food units per serve (3 pop-overs per serve)
2 PR = mince, egg
1 CB = flour
½ D = milk

Chicken Stroganoff

Serves 4
400 g (14 oz) chicken, diced
1 teaspoon olive oil
1 large onion, diced
1 clove garlic, minced
500 g (16 oz) mushrooms, sliced
1 red capsicum, cut into strips
375 ml (12 fl oz) light evaporated milk
1½ tablespoons cornflour
2 teaspoons wholegrain mustard
salt and freshly ground black pepper to taste
parsley to garnish
2 cups cooked pasta or rice

1 Sauté the chicken in the oil until cooked. Remove and set aside.

2 Add the onion and garlic to the pan and cook for 2 minutes. Add the mushrooms and capsicum and cook until tender.

3 Combine the milk, cornflour and mustard and add to the vegetables. Stir until thickened. Add the chicken and heat through. Season and serve over rice or pasta. Garnish with parsley.

Food units per serve
2 PR = chicken
1½ D = milk
1 CB = rice or pasta
25 Optional Indulgences = cornflour, oil

Chop Suey in a Jiffy

Serves 4
400 g (14 oz) mince, beef, chicken or pork
1 large onion, diced
2 large sticks celery, finely sliced
100 g (4 oz) green beans
2 large carrots, grated
250-300 g (8-10 oz) cabbage, shredded
2 packets 99% fat free chicken noodle soup
1 teaspoon curry powder
500 ml (18 fl oz) water

1   Brown the onions and mince in a non-stick fry pan, then sprinkle over the soup mix and curry powder.

2   Add the water and all the vegetables, bring to the boil and simmer for 15-20 minutes until the water has cooked away. Serve hot or cold on its own or with more noodles, rice or potato from your carbohydrate allowance.

Food units per serve
2 PR = mince
1 CB = any noodles/rice/potato
25 Optional Indulgences = soup mix

Country Chicken Pie

Serves 4
300 g (10 oz) chicken, diced small
75 g (3 oz) lean bacon, diced
2 cloves garlic, minced
1 teaspoon olive oil
1 large onion, sliced into rings
2 large carrots, diced small
100 g (4 oz) fresh or frozen peas
1 cup corn kernels
125 ml (4 fl oz) dry white wine
1-2 teaspoons dried mixed herbs
125 ml (4 fl oz) water
1 teaspoon chicken stock
125 ml (4 fl oz) low-fat unsweetened yoghurt
1 tablespoon cornflour
1 tablespoon light sour cream
salt and freshly ground black pepper to taste
6 sheets filo pastry

1 Sauté the chicken, bacon and garlic in the oil until browned, then remove and set aside.

2 Add the onions to the pan and cook until golden, then remove and set aside.

3 Add the carrots, peas, corn, wine, herbs, water and stock to the pan and simmer until the carrots are tender. Add the chicken into the pan and mix though the vegetables. Cool.

4 Mix the yoghurt, cornflour, sour cream, salt and pepper together. Add the yoghurt mix to the cooled chicken mix and vegetables.

5 Lightly spray a pie dish with cooking spray and layer sheets of filo across the dish. Place the sheets at different angles, so that you have some flowing over the edges to bring up on top of pie.

6 Spread the cooked onions over the filo, add the chicken and yoghurt mix. Pull the filo sheets over the mixture to form the top of the pie. Spray the top with a little cooking spray and bake in the oven at 180ºC for approximately 25 minutes or until the filo is brown and the filling is heated through.

Food units per serve
2 PR = chicken, bacon
1 CB = filo, corn
½ D = yoghurt
30 Optional Indulgences = cornflour, sour cream

Creamy Cheese Potato Bake

Serves 6
1 teaspoon butter
1 large onion, thinly sliced
2 cloves garlic, minced
900 g (30 oz) potato, sliced or diced small
500 g (16 oz) pumpkin, sliced or diced small
375 ml (12 fl oz) light evaporated milk
125 ml (4 fl oz) water
1 teaspoon chicken stock powder
2 tablespoons cornflour
75 g (3 oz) low-fat cheese, grated
salt and freshly ground black pepper to taste

1 Melt the butter in a pan and sauté the onions and garlic.

2 Remove from the heat and place on the base of a large oven-proof dish. Layer the potato and pumpkin in the dish on top of the onions.

3 Place the milk in a pan. Combine the water, chicken stock and cornflour and stir into the milk. Bring the milk to the boil, stirring constantly. Cook for 1-2 minutes over the heat, add half the cheese and stir through.

4 Remove from the heat and pour the sauce over the potato layer. Sprinkle with the remaining cheese and bake in the oven at 180ºC for approximately 1 hour or until the vegetables are cooked. (To save time you can pre-cook the vegetables in the microwave for 10 minutes.) Add salt and pepper to taste. Let the dish stand for 10 minutes before serving. This is great hot or cold.

Food units per serve
1 CB = potato
2 D = milk, cheese
20 Optional Indulgences = butter, cornflour

Creamy Chicken Satay Salad

Serves 4
300 g (10 oz) chicken, cooked and skinned
3 cups crunchy salad vegetables
salt and freshly ground black pepper to taste

Dressing
2 tablespoons crunchy peanut butter
2 tablespoons light sour cream
1 tablespoon low-fat mayonnaise
1 tablespoon sweet chilli sauce
125 ml (4 fl oz) low-fat unsweetened yoghurt

1 Combine the dressing ingredients together in a large bowl.

2 Add the vegetables and shredded chicken. Serve in lettuce leaves.

> This is a beautiful salad. It doesn't use any carbohydrates, which is good when you are trying to stretch out your food units for the day. You may like to serve it with a potato baked in its jacket.

Food units per serve
2 PR = chicken, peanut butter
$\frac{1}{2}$ D = yoghurt
15 Optional Indulgences = sour cream, mayonnaise

Creamy Smoked Chicken Pasta

Serves 4
1 teaspoon olive oil
4 cups of vegetables (eg carrot, zucchini, beans, capsicum, brussel sprouts)
1 large onion, sliced
375 ml (12 fl oz) light evaporated milk
1 tablespoon cornflour
3 teaspoons wholegrain mustard
salt to taste
50 g (2 oz) low-fat cheese
200 g (7 oz) smoked chicken
2 cups English spinach leaves, shredded
4 tablespoons parmesan cheese, grated
4 cups cooked pasta

1   Heat the oil in a pan, add all the vegetables except the spinach and cook for 2–3 minutes, or until just tender.

2   Combine the milk, cornflour, mustard, salt and low-fat cheese. Add to the vegetables and stir well while bringing to the boil. Add the chicken and spinach and cook for 2 minutes.

3   Pour over the hot cooked pasta, garnish with parmesan cheese and serve immediately.

Food units per serve
2 PR = cheeses, chicken
2 CB = pasta
2 D = milk
20 Optional Indulgences = cornflour, oil

Creamy Zucchini Risotto Bake

Serves 4
1 large onion, diced
2 cloves garlic, minced
1 green capsicum, finely diced
1 red capsicum, finely diced
500 ml (18 fl oz) hot water
1 cup arborio rice
500 ml (18 fl oz) low-fat milk
250 g (8 oz) mushrooms, sliced
2 large zucchini, grated and squeezed
2 eggs
75 g (3 oz) bacon, diced
4 tablespoons parmesan cheese, grated
2 teaspoons dried oregano
salt and freshly ground black pepper to taste

1   Cook the onion, garlic and capsicum in a small amount of water in a large pan until softened. Stir in the rice until well coated. Add the milk and water to the pan, cover and simmer until the rice is tender and the liquid is absorbed. (Keep an eye on it to make sure it does not stick.) Remove from the heat and allow to cool slightly.

2   Add the mushrooms, zucchini, eggs, bacon, cheese, oregano and salt and pepper. Pour into a baking dish and bake at 200°C for approximately 40 minutes or until set. Serve with salad.

> Some zucchini can be very watery. If you get a watery one, grate, sprinkle with salt and let it sit for 20 minutes. You can also squeeze them to get rid of some of the juices.

Food units per serve
2 PR = eggs, bacon, cheese
1 CB = rice
1 D = milk

Crusty Bread Bake

Serves 2
150 g (5 oz) crusty bread, cut into bite-sized pieces
3 medium tomatoes, thickly sliced
2 medium zucchini, sliced
1 red capsicum, diced
1 large onion, sliced
1 wedge pumpkin, peeled and diced
1 small eggplant, diced
2 cloves garlic, minced
2 tablespoons fresh herbs of your choice
100 g (4 oz) low-fat cheddar cheese
2 teaspoons olive oil
2 tablespoons sesame seeds to garnish

1   Mixed all the ingredients together in a bowl. Place in an oven-proof dish and bake at 180ºC for 30-40 minutes.

> This is a great way to use up stale bread. Serve with a green salad and a glass of red wine from your Optional Indulgences.

Food units per serve
2 PR = cheese
2 CB = bread
45 Optional Indulgences = oil

Curried Chicken Rice

Serves 4
300 g (10 oz) chicken, diced
1 teaspoon olive oil
1 onion, diced
2 cloves garlic, minced
1 large carrot, cut into matchsticks
100 g (4 oz) peas, frozen or fresh
1-3 teaspoons curry powder
2 cups brown rice, cooked
125 ml (4 fl oz) light evaporated milk
1 teaspoon coconut essence
2 tablespoons coriander, finely chopped (optional)
250 ml (8 fl oz) low-fat unsweetened yoghurt
1 tablespoon fresh mint, finely chopped
1 Lebanese cucumber, sliced
25 g (1 oz) slivered almonds, toasted

1 Sauté the chicken in the oil in a non-stick pan until browned, remove and set aside.

2 Add the onion, garlic, carrots, peas and curry powder to the pan. Stir until the vegetables are tender. Return the chicken to the pan and add the cooked rice. Mix together the milk and coconut essence, pour into the pan and stir through until the rice is hot. Stir in the coriander.

3 Mix the yoghurt, mint and cucumber together.

4 Serve the rice mixture garnished with almonds and topped with the yoghurt mixture.

> The amount of curry powder you should use depends on your taste and the quality of the powder. I often use Malaysian curry, which is available from Asian supermarkets.

Food units per serve
2 PR = chicken, almonds
1 CB = rice
1½ D = yoghurt, milk
10 Optional Indulgences = oil

Curried Lamb Stir-fry

Serves 4
200 g (7 oz) green beans, sliced
2 large carrots, cut into matchsticks
2 teaspoons sesame oil
2 teaspoons curry powder
2 cloves garlic, minced
400 g (14 oz) lamb, thinly sliced
1 cup snow peas
1 cup corn kernels, frozen or tinned
188 ml (6 fl oz) water
1 teaspoon chicken stock powder
1 tablespoon cornflour
2 teaspoons soy sauce

1 Lightly steam the beans and carrots.

2 Heat the sesame oil in a pan or wok, add the curry powder and garlic and stir-fry until fragrant.

3 Add the lamb and stir-fry until tender. Add all the vegetables and stir-fry until the peas are tender.

4 Blend together the water, stock, cornflour and soy sauce. Pour into the meat mixture and stir until it boils and thickens slightly. Serve.

> This dish has a wonderful flavour the day after it is made as the lamb and curry flavours blend together. It can be served with or without rice so it is an excellent dish if you are trying to save up carbohydrate units for a dinner out.

Food units per serve
2 PR = lamb
½ CB = corn
35 Optional Indulgences = oil, cornflour

Curried Pumpkin Pies

Serves 4

4 cups pumpkin, cooked and mashed
250 g (8 oz) frozen spinach, thawed and well drained
250 g (8 oz) cottage cheese
1 onion, diced
3 eggs
2 teaspoons curry powder
1 teaspoon chicken stock powder
75 g (3 oz) low-fat cheese, grated
6 sheets filo pasty

1 Combine all the ingredients except for the grated cheese and filo.

2 Use four individual pie dishes if you have them or a four serve pie dish. (If you are using individual dishes, cut the filo sheets in half to make 12 smaller sheets.) Spray the pie dish with cooking spray and layer 3 small sheets of filo across the dish. (Place the sheets at different angles so that the edges can be brought together to make the top of the pie.)

3 Divide the pumpkin mixture into four and place in the filo pie cases. Sprinkle a quarter of the grated cheese over each of the pies. Bake at 180°C for approximately 25 minutes or until the filo is brown.

This dish can be served with Baked Vegetables (page 77).

Food units per serve
2 PR = eggs, cottage cheese and part of the grated cheese
½ CB = filo
1 D = the rest of the grated cheese

Devilled Potatoes

Serves 2

600 g (20 oz) washed potatoes, peeled or unpeeled
3 or more cups firm vegetables (use ones that hold their shape when cooked, eg celery, carrots)
410 g (14 oz) tinned diced tomatoes
2 teaspoons golden syrup
1 teaspoon prepared mild mustard
2 tablespoons white wine (optional)
salt and freshly ground black pepper to taste
4 tablespoons parmesan cheese, grated
25 g (1 oz) low-fat cheese, grated

1   Dice or slice potatoes into 2.5 cm (1 inch) pieces.

2   Combine all the other remaining ingredients except the cheese. Lightly spray an oven-proof dish with cooking spray. Pour in mixture. Sprinkle the cheese on top and bake at 180ºC for 35-45 minutes or until the potatoes are cooked.

Food units per serve
1 PR = parmesan
2 CB = potato
1 D = cheese
15 Optional Indulgences = golden syrup

Ezy Bacon and Egg Pie

Serves 4
4 eggs
125 ml (4 fl oz) low-fat unsweetened yoghurt
1 tablespoon cornflour
50 g (2 oz) fresh or frozen peas
salt and freshly ground black pepper to taste
6 sheets filo pastry
1 tablespoon tomato sauce
1 small onion, finely chopped
160 g (5 oz) bacon, chopped (all fat removed)
1-2 large tomatoes, chopped and de-seeded

1 Combine the eggs, yoghurt and cornflour in a bowl. Add the peas, salt and pepper.

2 Place the sheets of filo across a pie dish at different angles. Spread the tomato sauce over the base, sprinkle the onions over the sauce, then the bacon. Pour over the egg mixture. Sprinkle with tomatoes.

3 Bring the edges of the filo sheets over the top of the pie, spray with cooking spray and bake at 180°C for 30 minutes or until the egg has set. This is delicious hot or cold.

Food units per serve
2 PR = bacon, eggs
½ CB = filo
½ D = yoghurt
20 Optional Indulgences = cornflour, tomato sauce

5-Minute Singapore Noodles

Serves 2
80 g (2½ oz) 99% fat free 2-minute noodles
250 ml (8 fl oz) water
1 teaspoon sesame oil
200 g (7 oz) chicken, diced
1 clove garlic, minced
1 teaspoon root ginger, finely sliced (optional)
1 onion, diced
500 g (16 oz) frozen stir-fry vegetables
soy sauce to taste

1   Microwave noodles in water for 2 minutes on high (or cover with boiling water and sit for 5 minutes). Drain off the excess water.

2   Sauté the chicken, garlic, ginger and onion in the sesame oil for a couple of minutes. Add frozen vegetables and stir-fry until nearly cooked. Add the noodles, flavour sachet and soy sauce and stir through. Serve immediately.

Food units per serve
2 PR = chicken
1½ CB = noodles
20 Optional Indulgences = oil

Five Spice Beef

Serves 2
200 g (7oz) beef, thinly sliced
1 clove garlic, minced
1 teaspoon fresh ginger root, grated
½ teaspoon Chinese five spice powder
1 teaspoon peanut oil
2 cups broccoli florets, lightly steamed
2 large carrots, cut into matchsticks and lightly steamed
½ teaspoon salt
1 tablespoon soy sauce
125 ml (4 fl oz) boiling water
2 teaspoons cornflour
1 tablespoon cold water
2 cups cooked rice

1 Place the beef in a plastic bag. Mix the garlic, ginger and five spice powder together then toss with the beef.

2 Heat the oil in a pan or wok. Stir-fry the beef for 3 minutes, then add in the broccoli, carrots, salt, soy sauce and hot water and heat to simmering point.

3 Mix the cornflour with cold water, add to the beef, stirring until it boils and thickens. Serve over boiled rice.

When using fresh ginger root, peel and grate it. Any excess can be frozen. It has a wonderful full flavour when compared with the bottled variety. This is such an easy recipe to prepare and the rich green of the broccoli looks wonderful against the spiced beef.

Food units per serve
2 PR = beef
2 CB = rice
20 Optional Indulgences = oil, cornflour

Ham and Cheese Pancakes

Serves 4
3 large zucchini, grated
salt and freshly ground black pepper to taste
1 cup self-raising flour
1 egg
125–188 ml (4–6 fl oz) low-fat milk
100 g (4 oz) ham, finely diced
1 cup corn kernels
50 g (2 oz) low-fat cheese, grated
chilli powder to taste

1 After grating the zucchini, sprinkle with salt and let stand for 20 minutes. Drain and squeeze out any excess juice.

2 Combine the flour, egg and milk to make a batter. Add all the remaining ingredients and stir through.

3 Spoon onto a non-stick pan or barbeque. Cook until the mixture bubbles, then turn over and cook the other side. (You may need to use a non-stick cooking spray.)

4 Serve hot or cold with a side salad.

These are great little pancakes to serve in the winter with a bowl of piping hot soup.

Food units per serve
1½ PR = cheese, ham, egg
1½ CB = flour, corn
½ D = milk

Ham and Cheese Pie

Serves 2

4 slices multigrain bread, crumbled
1 small onion, finely diced
1 teaspoon garlic, minced
2 tablespoons low-fat unsweetened yoghurt
50 g (2 oz) ham or pastrami, diced
3 large tomatoes, skinned, de-seeded and diced
2 tablespoons plain flour
250 ml (8 fl oz) low-fat milk
50 g (2 oz) low-fat cheese, grated
4 tablespoons parmesan cheese, grated

1 Mix the bread, onion, garlic and yoghurt together into a paste and line a pie dish with the mixture. Be careful not to make the mixture too sticky.

2 Spread the ham and tomatoes over the bread base.

3 Mix the flour with a little milk and stir through the remaining milk. Heat the milk and flour mixture, stirring constantly until the milk thickens. Add the grated cheese and stir through.

4 Pour over the ham and tomatoes. Sprinkle the parmesan cheese over the top and bake for 30 minutes on 180°C. Serve hot or cold.

Food units per serve
2 PR = ham, cheese
2 CB = bread
2 D = milk, cheese
10 Optional Indulgences = yoghurt

Ham and Tomato Pasta Bake

Serves 2

4 large tomatoes, peeled and diced
1 large onion, diced
2 zucchini, sliced
1 tablespoon oregano fresh or 1 teaspoon dried
2 cloves garlic, minced
1 tablespoon soy sauce
2 eggs
125 ml (4 fl oz) low-fat unsweetened yoghurt
1 teaspoon wholegrain mustard
1 teaspoon cornflour
salt and freshly ground black pepper to taste
100 g (4 oz) ham, diced
50 g (2 oz) low-fat cheese, grated
2 cups cooked pasta

1 Sauté the vegetables, herbs and soy sauce for 2–3 minutes.

2 Beat together the eggs, yoghurt and mustard, cornflour and seasonings.
Add the ham, vegetables and pasta to the egg mixture and stir through.

3 Place in a greased oven-proof dish. Sprinkle with the cheese and bake at
180°C for approximately 45 minutes. Let the dish stand for 10 minutes,
then serve warm or cold.

> Peel tomatoes by piercing the skin and then plunging into a bowl of boiling water
> for 30–40 seconds. Remove from the water and peel.

Food units per serve
2 PR = eggs, ham
2 CB = pasta
2½ D = yoghurt, cheese

Ham, Cheese and Pineapple Pizza

Serves 2

4 slices wholemeal or multigrain bread, crumbed
1 small onion, finely diced
2 tablespoons low-fat unsweetened yoghurt
2 tablespoons plain flour
250 ml (8 fl oz) low-fat milk
50 g (2 oz) low-fat cheese, grated
salt and freshly ground black pepper to taste
2 tablespoons tomato sauce
1 teaspoon prepared mustard
2 spring onions, sliced
100 g (4 oz) ham, diced
100 g (4 oz) pineapple, crushed
2 tomatoes, sliced

1   Mix the bread, onion and yoghurt together until it starts to form a paste. Be careful you do not make the mixture too sticky. Lightly spray a quiche dish with cooking spray and line the dish with the bread mixture.

2   Combine the flour and a little milk, then stir in the remaining milk and heat until the mixture thickens. Add the grated cheese. Season.

3   Mix the tomato sauce and mustard together and spread over the bread base. Layer the spring onions, ham and pineapple, then pour over the milk sauce. Garnish with sliced tomato. Bake at 180°C for 20-25 minutes. Serve hot or cold.

> **This dish makes finger food at a party.**

Food units per serve
2 PR = ham, cheese
2 CB = bread
$^{1}/_{2}$ F = pineapple
1 D = milk, yoghurt
55 Optional Indulgences = tomato sauce, flour

Honey Sesame Chicken Stir-fry

Serves 4
400 g (14 oz) chicken, diced
1 clove garlic, minced
2 tablespoons soy sauce
2 tablespoons red wine
2 teaspoons honey
2 teaspoons sesame oil
3 spring onions, sliced
1 teaspoon fresh ginger, finely diced
2 large carrots, cut into matchsticks
1 bunch fresh asparagus or broccoli
2 tablespoons sesame seeds, toasted in microwave for 30 seconds
125 ml (4 fl oz) water
1 teaspoon cornflour
2 cups cooked rice

1 Marinate the chicken in garlic, soy, wine and honey for at least 30 minutes.

2 Drain the chicken and save the marinade. Heat the sesame oil in a wok or pan and stir-fry the drained chicken until cooked. Remove the chicken and set aside.

3 Add the spring onions and ginger to a pan and stir-fry for 30 seconds or until aromatic. Add the carrots and asparagus and stir-fry for 2-3 minutes. Add the sesame seeds. Return the chicken to a pan with the reserved marinade. Stir through.

4 Combine the cornflour and water and add to the pan, stirring until thickened. Remove and serve.

This dish is also nice with a jacket potato.

Food units per serve.
2 PR = chicken
1 CB = rice
35 Optional Indulgences = oil, honey, cornflour

Indian Curry Chicken

Serves 4
400 g (14 oz) chicken, diced
1 teaspoon olive oil
1 large onion, diced
1 clove garlic, minced
1 tablespoon curry powder
2 teaspoons sweet paprika
1 teaspoons ground coriander
1 teaspoon ground cumin
½ tablespoon ground cloves
375 ml (12 fl oz) light evaporated milk
1 tablespoon cornflour
125 ml (4 fl oz) water
1 red capsicum, diced
1 large carrot, cut into matchsticks
100 g (4 oz) frozen peas
4 cups cooked rice
125 ml (4 fl oz) low-fat unsweetened yoghurt
salt to taste

1 Heat the oil in a pan, add the chicken and brown. Remove and set aside. Add the onion and garlic to the pan and cook for 2 minutes.

2 Add the curry powder, paprika, coriander, cumin and cloves. Cook, stirring for approximately 1 minute.

3 Combine the milk, cornflour, water and salt. Add to the pan and bring slowly to the boil, stirring constantly. Add the capsicum, carrot, peas and chicken and simmer for 10 minutes. Serve over steamed rice. Top with a spoonful of yoghurt and enjoy!

Food units per serve
2 PR = chicken
1 CB = rice
2 D = milk, yoghurt

Lavish Bread Chips

1 serve
1 packet pita pocket bread or lavish bread
cooking spray

Add any of the following toppings
minced garlic
cajun spice
chicken stock powder
garlic salt
chilli powder
lemon pepper

1 Preheat the oven to 200°C.

2 Split each pita round in half and spray the bread with cooking spray. Sprinkle with topping.

3 Bake in the oven for 5-8 minutes until browned. Remove, cool and break up into chips. (You can cut the bread into triangles if you prefer before cooking.)

or

1 Split each round in half and spray the bread with cooking spray. Sprinkle with topping.

2 Place the bread into the microwave and cook on high for one minute or until crisp.

These are a wonderful alternative to high fat, high calorie potato chips. They are simple to make and great to nibble on if you get the munchies. There may be other 'free toppings' you could try, but remember that if you are using parmesan cheese, you must count it under your protein, dairy or optional units.

These could also be served with recipes from the Soups and Dips section.

Food units per Lavish or pita bread
2 CB = pita or Lavish bread

Lemon Chicken and Cheese Pies

Serves 2
125 ml (4 fl oz) water
1 teaspoon chicken stock powder
1 tablespoon cornflour
juice of half a lemon
1 tablespoon light sour cream
50 g (2 oz) low-fat cheese, grated
2 large zucchini, finely diced
100 g (4 oz) chicken, diced
3 sheets filo pastry
salt and freshly ground black pepper to taste

1 Heat the water, chicken stock and cornflour until thickened, then add the lemon juice. Stir through the sour cream, cheese, zucchini and seasonings and cool. Add the chicken.

2 Take one sheet of filo and cut it in half. Spray a single serve pie dish with cooking spray and place one full sheet of filo across it and another half sheet in the middle. Place half the mixture in the pie dish and bring the sides of filo up over the top to form a frilly pie top.

3 Repeat with the other pie. Lightly spray the tops of the pies with cooking spray. Bake at 180°C for 35-40 minutes or until the filo is browned. Stand for 5 minutes to allow the sauce inside to thicken. Serve with steamed green vegetables or a salad.

> Notice this recipe only uses half a CB unit - you could have a baked potato with it if you wished.

Food units per serve
2 PR = cheese, chicken
½ CB = filo
40 Optional Indulgences = cornflour, sour cream

Lite Caesar Salad

Serves 4
80 g (3 oz) lean bacon
8 slices slices French bread stick 2.5 cm (1 inch) thick
4 teaspoons parmesan cheese, grated
2 eggs, hardboiled, cut into quarters
lots of crisp lettuce leaves

Dressing
4 anchovy fillets
1 egg
125 g (4½ oz) smooth cottage cheese
65 ml (2 fl oz) low-fat unsweetened yoghurt
1 tablespoon lemon juice
1 teaspoon lemon zest
1-2 teaspoons garlic, minced

1 Grill the bacon, cool and chop into bite-size pieces.

2 Place the bread slices on an oven tray, spray with cooking spray and sprinkle over the parmesan cheese. Bake at 200ºC until browned, approximately 5-10 minutes. Cool and break in half.

3 Mix the salad ingredients together and add the french stick croutons.

4 Blend the dressing ingredients together until smooth. Season and pour over the salad. Serve immediately.

> The dressing will thicken while standing, so if you have the time it is a good idea to let it sit for a couple of hours. The recipe makes approximately 500 ml (16 fl oz) and will keep for about a week. (1 tablespoon = 20 Optional)

Food units per serve
1½ PR = bacon, eggs, parmesan, anchovy, egg
½ CB = French stick
1 D = yoghurt, cheese

Macaroni Magic

Serves 2
150 g (5 oz) very lean beef mince
1 medium onion, diced
½ teaspoon curry powder
1 clove garlic, minced
410 g (14 oz) tinned diced tomatoes
1 tablespoon tomato paste
pinch dried mixed herbs
1 teaspoon Worcestershire sauce
salt and freshly ground black pepper to taste
65 ml (2 fl oz) water
75 g (2½ oz) low-fat cheese, grated
1 cup cooked macaroni pasta
1 slice bread (day old, stale) crumbed

1　Sauté the mince, onion, curry powder and garlic in a non-stick pan.

2　Add the tomatoes, paste, herbs, Worcestershire sauce, salt, pepper and water. Bring to the boil. Stir in half of the cheese and heat gently until the cheese is melted.

3　Fold the macaroni through the mixture and place in a casserole dish.

4　Combine the remaining cheese and breadcrumbs and sprinkle over the mince mixture. Bake at 180ºC for approximately 30 minutes. Serve with a salad or steamed green vegetables.

Food units per serve
2 PR = mince, cheese
1½ CB = pasta, bread
2 D = cheese
50 Optional Indulgences = tomato paste

Muffin with Baked Beans

Serves 1

½ cup baked beans in tomato sauce

1 English muffin

2 slices low-fat cheese

1 Cut muffin in half. Heat baked beans and toast muffin.

2 Place 1 slice of cheese onto each half muffin and top with beans. Serve.

Food units per serve

1 PR = baked beans

1½ CB = muffin

2 D = cheese

Mushroom and Bacon Risotto

Serves 2
80 g (3 oz) lean bacon, diced
1 onion, diced
1 clove garlic, minced
1 cup arborio rice
125 ml (4 fl oz) dry white wine
1 teaspoon chicken stock
500 ml (18 fl oz) boiling water
250 g (8 oz) mushrooms, sliced
50 g (2 oz) frozen peas
2 tablespoons parmesan cheese, grated
1 tablespoon light sour cream
salt and freshly ground black pepper to taste
2 large tomatoes, diced

1 Sauté the bacon, onion and garlic in a non-stick pan until limp. Add the rice.

2 Add the wine, stock and water. Cover and simmer until the rice is cooked (You may need to add more water.)

3 Stir through the mushroom and peas and cook for 5 minutes.

4 Stir in the cheese, sour cream, salt and pepper. Add the tomatoes, stir through and serve.

> Arborio is a risotto rice which is quick to cook and makes a lovely, creamy risotto.

Food units per serve
2 PR = bacon, cheese
2 CB = rice
20 Optional Indulgences = sour cream

One Pot Beef and Noodles

Serves 2
200 g (7 oz) lean beef mince
2 cloves garlic, minced
2 large sticks celery, finely diced
1 red capsicum, diced
1 large onion, diced
3 tablespoons vinegar
375 ml (12 fl oz) water
1 teaspoon all spice
1 teaspoon beef stock powder
30 g (1 oz) raisins, chopped
375 g (12 oz) cabbage, shredded
1 cup fresh noodles
salt and freshly ground black pepper to taste

1 Sauté the mince, garlic, celery, capsicum and onion in a non-stick pan until almost cooked.

2 Mix the vinegar, water, all spice and beef stock and add to the meat mixture.

3 Add the raisins, cabbage and noodles, stirring until cooked through (you may need to add extra water). Season and serve.

Food units per serve
2 PR = beef
1 CB = noodles
½ F = raisins

Oriental Barbecue Patties

Serves 4
350 g (12 oz) lean beef or chicken mince
1 onion, finely diced
1 clove garlic, minced
1 zucchini, grated
1 small red capsicum, finely chopped
2 slices day-old wholemeal bread, crumbed
1 tablespoon hoi sin sauce
1 egg, lightly beaten
salt and freshly ground black pepper to taste

1 Mix all the ingredients together.

2 Form the mixture into small patties (12-16). Lightly spray the barbeque or frypan with cooking spray and cook the patties.

3 Serve hot or cold with a generous serve of Tomato and Coriander Salsa (page 162).

These are great to keep and eat the next day, and could even go inside a pita pocket for lunch.

Food units per serve
2 PR = mince, egg
$\frac{1}{2}$ CB or 50 Optional Indulgences = bread

Pasta Carbonara

Serves 4
400 g (14 oz) mushrooms, sliced
1 large onion, diced
160 g (5 oz) lean bacon or 200 g (7 oz) pastrami
250 ml (8 fl oz) evaporated milk
8 sun-dried or dehydrated tomatoes, diced
1 tablespoon light sour cream
4 tablespoons parmesan cheese, grated
freshly ground black pepper
4 cups pasta, cooked

1 Reconstitute the dried tomatoes in boiling water for 5 minutes.

2 Sauté the mushrooms in a non-stick pan until just tender (they can cook in their own juices). Remove and set aside.

3 Add the onion and bacon to a pan and sauté until golden brown. Pour the evaporated milk over the mixture and simmer for 5 minutes.

4 Add the diced sun-dried tomatoes (drained) and the mushrooms, and heat through.

5 Stir through the sour cream and cheese. Add the pasta and toss, season and serve.

> Pastrami is very lean beef, chicken or turkey with a strong flavour and can be found in the supermarket in the deli department. You can buy it by the gram.

Food units per serve
1½ PR = bacon, parmesan cheese
2 CB = pasta
1 D = milk
10 Optional Indulgences = sour cream

Pasta with Pork Strips

Serves 2
200 g (7 oz) pork, cut into strips
1 onion, diced
1 clove garlic, minced
1 teaspoon olive oil
410 g (14 oz) tinned diced tomatoes
1 tablespoon honey
1 teaspoon dried oregano
1 teaspoon red chilli,
2 large zucchini, sliced
¼ cup fresh basil, finely chopped
salt and freshly ground black pepper to taste
2 cups pasta, cooked

1 Sauté the pork, onion and garlic in the oil in a non-stick pan until browned.

2 Add tomatoes, honey, oregano, chilli and zucchini. Simmer for 10 minutes. Add the chopped basil. Season and serve over your favourite hot pasta.

Food units per serve
2 PR = pork
2 CB = pasta
30 Optional Indulgences = honey

Pastrami and Pumpkin Risotto

Serves 2
1 onion, diced
1 clove garlic, minced
1 teaspoon olive oil
1 cup arborio rice
125 ml (4 fl oz) dry white wine
2 teaspoons chicken stock powder
500 ml (18 fl oz) boiling water
2 cups pumpkin, cooked and mashed
50 g (2 oz) pastrami
3 spring onions, diced
50 g (2 oz) low-fat cheese, grated
1 tablespoon light sour cream
salt and freshly ground black pepper to taste

1   Sauté the onion and garlic in the oil until limp. Add the rice and stir until the rice is covered in oil.

2   Add the wine, stock and water. Cover and simmer until the rice is cooked. (More water may be added if it is needed.)

3   Stir through the pumpkin, pastrami and spring onions. Simmer until these are warmed through. Add the cheese, sour cream, salt and pepper, and serve.

Food units per serve
2 PR = pastrami, cheese
2 CB = rice
40 Optional Indulgences = oil, sour cream

Perfect Pizza

Serves 4 (makes 4 individual pizzas or 1 large one)

Base
2 cups self-raising flour
1 sachet dried yeast
½ teaspoon sugar
½ teaspoon salt
lukewarm water

Topping (per individual pizza)
1 tablespoon tomato sauce
1 tablespoon Worcestershire sauce
80 g (3 oz) bacon, diced
1 red capsicum, roasted and diced
1 green capsicum, diced
1 large onion, finely diced
1 large tomato, skinned and diced
sprinkle of oregano
50 g (2 oz) low-fat cheese, grated

1 Preheat the oven to 180°C.

2 Combine all the dry ingredients for the base and mix together. Add enough water to form a dough and knead well. Cover with plastic wrap and leave in a warm place until the dough has doubled in size. Punch the dough down and knead again. (You may add a sprinkle of flour if it is needed.) If you are making small pizzas, divide the dough into four sections.

3 Roll out the dough and place it on greased oven trays.

4 Combine the tomato and Worcestershire sauces and spread over the base. Place the bacon, vegetables and oregano over the sauces, sprinkle with cheese and bake in the oven for approximately 20 minutes.

Food units per serve
2 PR = bacon
2 CB = flour
2D = cheese

Pork and Cashew Stir-fry

Serves 4
200 g (7 oz) pork, finely diced
2 teaspoons garlic, minced
1 teaspoon peanut oil
1 onion, diced
½ green capsicum, diced
½ red capsicum, diced
½ yellow capsicum, diced
2 large carrots, cut into matchsticks
snow peas to taste
60 g (2 oz) cashew nuts, roasted
2 cups hokkien noodles, pre-cooked

Sauce
2 tablespoons fish sauce
2 tablespoons oyster sauce
1 teaspoon brown sugar
2 teaspoons cornflour
2 teaspoons chicken stock powder
125 ml (4 fl oz) water

1 Mix the sauce ingredients together.

2 Stir-fry the pork and garlic in the oil in a frypan or wok until cooked. Remove and set aside.

3 Add the onion, capsicum and carrot to the pan and stir-fry until tender. Return the pork to the pan and add the sauce. Stir until thickened. Add the snow peas, cashews and noodles and stir until heated through. Serve.

To roast cashews place in a microwave for approximately 30 seconds (make sure they don't burn), or stir-fry in a pan until golden brown.

Hokkien noodles can be found in the refrigerator section of your supermarket. ($\frac{1}{2}$ cup = 50 g (2 oz) = 1 CB)

Food units per serve
2 PR = pork, cashews
1 CB = noodles
20 Optional Indulgences = oil, sugar, cornflour

Pork and Mushroom Risotto

Serves 4
1 large onion, diced
3 cloves garlic, minced
350 g (12 oz) pork, cut into strips
1 fresh red chilli, de-seeded and diced
1 teaspoon olive oil
1 cup arborio rice
125 ml (4 fl oz) dry white wine
1 litre (36 fl oz) boiling water
2 teaspoons chicken stock powder
400 g (14 oz) mushrooms, sliced
1 red capsicum, diced
4 tablespoons parmesan cheese, grated
1 tablespoon light sour cream
¼ cup parsley, finely chopped
freshly ground black pepper to taste

1 Sauté the onion, garlic, pork and chilli in the oil until the pork is browned. Add the rice and stir until it is covered in oil.

2 Add the wine, boiling water and stock and cook until the rice is tender. (You can add a little more water if it is needed.) Add the mushrooms and capsicum and cook until the vegetables are tender. Add the cheese, sour cream and parsley, and season with pepper. Serve.

Take care to wash your hands well after handling the chilli.

Food units per serve
2 PR = pork, cheese
1 CB = rice
15 Optional Indulgences = oil, sour cream

Pork and Pear Stir-fry

Serves 2
200 g (7 oz) pork, finely sliced
1 teaspoon olive oil
3 spring onions, thinly sliced
½ teaspoon garlic, minced
½ teaspoon ginger, finely diced or minced
100 g (4 oz) snow peas, trimmed
½ cup tinned pears in natural juice, sliced
1 tablespoon sweet chilli sauce
2 tablespoons soy sauce
2 tablespoons water
1 teaspoon cornflour
2 cups cooked rice

1 Sauté the pork in the oil until browned. Add the spring onions, garlic and ginger, and stir-fry for approximately 1 minute.

2 Add the snow peas and pears. Combine the sauces, water and cornflour. Add to the pork and stir-fry for 5 minutes or until the snow peas are tender and the pork is cooked. Serve over rice.

Food units per serve
2 PR = pork
2 CB = rice
½ F = pears
25 Optional Indulgences = oil, cornflour

Potato and Cheese Parcels

Serves 2
300 g (10 oz) potato, peeled and grated
1 large carrot, grated
300 g (10 oz) pumpkin, grated
1 onion, finely diced
1 teaspoon dried sage
1 tablespoon cornflour
1 tablespoon sweet chilli sauce
100 g (4 oz) low-fat cheese, grated
6 sheets filo pastry
salt and freshly ground black pepper to taste

1   Mix all the ingredients together except the filo pastry.

2   Lay three sheets of filo on top of each other. Place half the mixture down at one end of the sheets. Roll the filo over the mixture once and then tuck the sides in. Continue rolling the filo to the end. Repeat with the other half of the mixture.

3   Lightly spray an oven tray with cooking spray. Place the parcels on this tray and lightly spray the top of each parcel. Bake in the oven at 170°C for 35-40 minutes or until the filo is browned and the potato is cooked. Serve with steamed green vegetables or a salad.

Food units per serve
2 PR = cheese
2 CB = potato, filo
20 Optional Indulgences = cornflour

Pumpkin and Bean Risotto

Serves 4
1 large onion, sliced
2 cloves garlic, minced
400 g (14 oz) pumpkin, diced
1 teaspoon olive oil
1 cup arborio rice
500 ml boiling water
2 teaspoons beef stock powder
400 g (14 oz) tinned borlotti beans, rinsed and drained
80 g (3 oz) bacon, diced and cooked
2 tablespoons parmesan cheese, grated
1 tablespoon light sour cream

1 Sauté the onion, garlic and pumpkin in the oil for a few minutes. Add the rice and stir until it is covered in oil.

2 Add the boiling water and stock and cook until the rice is tender. (You may add a little more water if it is needed.)

3 Add the beans and bacon and heat through. Stir through the cheese and sour cream and serve.

Food units per serve
2 PR = beans, bacon, cheese
1 CB = rice
20 Optional Indulgences = oil, sour cream

Pumpkin and Feta Filo Parcels

Serves 2
2 cups pumpkin, diced
1 teaspoon chicken stock powder
2 large leeks, sliced
1 teaspoon butter
½ teaspoon chilli powder
50 g (2 oz) feta cheese
6 sheets filo pastry

1 Cover the pumpkin with water and add the chicken stock. Cook until the pumpkin is soft, then drain and mash.

2 Sauté the leeks in butter until soft and wilted. Add the pumpkin and chilli powder. Cool.

3 Lay three sheets of filo on top of each other. Place half the pumpkin mixture at one end and crumble half the feta cheese over the top of the pumpkin. Fold the filo sheet over the mixture once, then tuck in the sides. Continue to roll up the filo sheets. Repeat to make a second parcel.

4 Lightly spray an oven-proof dish or tray with cooking spray. Place the parcels on the tray and lightly spray the top of each parcel then scatter with sesame seeds, poppy seeds or chilli powder. Bake for approximately 30 minutes at 180°C or until browned. Serve with a salad or steamed green vegetables.

Food units per serve
1 PR or 2 D = cheese
1 CB = filo
20 Optional Indulgences = butter

Pumpkin Penne

Serves 4
1 onion, diced
2 cloves garlic, minced
80 g (3 oz) bacon, diced
1 teaspoon olive oil
4 cups pumpkin, cooked and mashed
125 ml (4 fl oz) boiling water
1 teaspoon chicken stock powder
50 g (2 oz) low-fat cheese, grated
2 tablespoons light sour cream
chilli powder to taste
salt and freshly ground black pepper to taste
4 tablespoons parmesan cheese, grated
2 spring onions, finely sliced for garnish
2 cups cooked penne pasta

1 Sauté the onion, garlic and bacon in the oil in a non-stick pan until browned.

2 Add mashed pumpkin, boiling water and chicken stock, and stir until the onions are tender.

3 Add the grated cheese, sour cream, chilli and seasonings, and stir through. Garnish with the parmesan cheese and spring onions and serve over the cooked pasta.

Food units per serve
2 PR = bacon, cheeses
1 CB = pasta
20 Optional Indulgences = oil, sour cream

Rich Beef Stroganoff

Serves 4
400 g (14 oz) lean beef, cubed
1 tablespoon cornflour
2 large onions, halved and sliced
2 cloves garlic, minced
1 teaspoon olive oil
500 g (16 oz) mushrooms, sliced
1 teaspoon beef stock powder
125 ml (4 fl oz) water
2 tablespoons tomato paste with garlic and herbs
820 g (27 oz) tinned diced tomatoes
salt and freshly ground black pepper to taste
splash of red wine
125 ml (4 fl oz) low-fat unsweetened yoghurt
2 tablespoons light sour cream
4 cups cooked pasta

1 Place the beef and cornflour in a plastic bag and shake together.

2 Sauté the onion and garlic in the oil and add the meat. Cook until browned, then add the mushrooms. Stir for a few minutes until the mushrooms are cooked.

3 Combine the water and beef stock. Add the tomato paste, tomatoes, seasonings and red wine, and bring to the boil. Turn down and simmer for 10-15 minutes, stirring occasionally until the mixture thickens.

4 Mix the yoghurt and sour cream and stir through the stroganoff. Serve over the cooked pasta.

Food units per serve
2 PR = beef
2 CB = pasta
$\frac{1}{2}$ D = yoghurt
35 Optional Indulgences = flour, oil, paste, sour cream

Roast Capsicum Pesto

Serves 4

3 large red capsicums, de-seeded
4 tablespoons parmesan cheese,
grated zest of ½ lemon
2 cloves garlic, minced
125 ml (4 fl oz) low-fat unsweetened yoghurt
1 tablespoon balsamic vinegar
1 tablespoon light sour cream
salt and freshly ground black pepper to taste

1 Cut the capsicums into quarters and place them on a tray under the griller. Leave until the skin bubbles and blackens and starts to lift off. Remove and cool a little. Hold the capsicum pieces under running cold water then peel the skin off.

2 Blend all the ingredients together and serve over pasta or baked vegetables (page 77).

If you choose to serve over pasta, remember to count this as part of your daily carbohydrate food units.

Balsamic vinegar is available from most markets and supermarkets. It is a red wine vinegar and wonderful for salad dressings.

Food units per serve
1 PR = cheese
½ D = yoghurt
10 Optional Indulgences = sour cream

Salmon and Asparagus Crepe Stack

Serves 4
210 g (7 oz) tinned salmon, drained
1 onion, diced
1 tin asparagus, drained
125 g (4½ oz) cottage cheese
125 ml (4 fl oz) low-fat unsweetened yoghurt
1 tablespoon cornflour
1 tablespoon light sour cream
1 tablespoon lemon juice
2 tablespoons white wine
salt and freshly ground black pepper to taste
8 crepes

Topping
75 g low-fat cheese, grated
125 ml (4 fl oz) low-fat unsweetened yoghurt
1 egg

1 Combine the topping ingredients.

2 Combine all the other ingredients in a separate bowl except for the crepes.

3 Take two crepes and immerse them briefly in warm water. Remove immediately. Shake the excess water off and lay the crepes flat in a square pie dish. Spread a third of the mixture on top of the crepes. Repeat until the mixture is finished.

4 Bake in the oven at 180°C for 25-30 minutes. Serve with a green salad or steamed vegetables.

Look for crepes that have a calorie count of around 50 calories per crepe. You should also check the manufacturer's instructions for use. Some may not need to be immersed in water.

Food units per serve
2 PR = salmon, cheeses
1 CB = crepes
1 D = yoghurt
20 Optional Indulgences = cornflour, sour cream

Salmon Quiche

Serves 4
1 cup self-raising flour
375 ml (12 fl oz) low-fat milk
4 eggs
210 g (7 oz) salmon
3 cups broccoli, lightly steamed
1 onion, diced
3 large tomatoes, de-seeded and diced
2 tablespoons lemon juice
salt and freshly ground black pepper to taste
75 g low-fat cheese, grated

1 Combine the flour, milk and eggs together with a whisk.

2 Add the remaining ingredients except the cheese, and mix together. Lightly spray a quiche dish with cooking spray and pour in the mixture. Sprinkle the cheese over the top.

3 Bake at 200°C for approximately 45 minutes. Serve hot or cold.

This dish can also be made using tuna.

Food units used per serve
2 PR = egg, salmon, cheese
1 CB = flour
1 D = milk, cheese

Savoury Cheese Muffins

Serves 12
1 large onion, diced
125 ml (4 fl oz) cup low-fat milk
3 eggs
75 g (3 oz) low-fat cheese
1 cup corn kernels (include a little juice)
2 large carrots, grated
2 tablespoons parsley, finely chopped
2½ cups self-raising flour
1 teaspoon baking powder
pinch of chilli powder
salt and freshly ground black pepper to taste

1   Mix the onion, milk, eggs, cheese, corn, carrot and parsley together.

2   Add the flour, baking powder, chilli and salt and pepper, and mix together well.

3   Lightly spray a muffin tin with cooking spray and place the mixture in the moulds. Bake at 200°C for 25-30 minutes. Serve hot or cold.

Food units per serve
Each muffin
1 CB = flour, corn
½ D = milk, cheese
20 Optional Indulgences = eggs

Savoury Fritters

Serves 2

½ cup self-raising flour
1 egg
125 ml (4 fl oz) low-fat milk
40 g (1½ oz) bacon or pastrami, finely diced
1 cup creamed sweet corn
1 small onion, finely diced
1 tomato, skinned and de-seeded, finely diced
chives or parsley, finely chopped
salt and freshly ground black pepper to taste
chilli or curry powder to taste

1 Combine the flour, egg and milk.

2 Add the remaining ingredients and stir through.

3 Place spoonfuls of the mixture in a non-stick pan or barbeque. Cook until the mixture bubbles, then turn the fritter over and cook the other side. (You may need to lightly spray the pan or barbeque with cooking spray before cooking.) Serve hot or cold with tomato salsa or a serve of Tomato Dip (page 73).

To skin a tomato easily, plunge tomato into boiling water for 30 seconds. Remove the tomato and pierce skin with knife. The skin should peel back easily. If it doesn't, return to the water and try again. Be careful not to burn yourself.

Food units per serve
1 PR = egg, bacon
2 CB = flour, corn
½ D = milk

Savoury Rice

Serves 4
2 cloves garlic, minced
1 large onion, diced
100 g (4 oz) pastrami, diced
1 teaspoon olive oil
1 cup rice
410 g tinned diced tomatoes in juice
2 cups vegetables of your choice
375 ml (12 fl oz) water
salt and freshly ground black pepper to taste

1 Sauté the garlic, onion and pastrami in the oil for a few minutes. Stir in the rice until it is coated with the oil.

2 Add the tomatoes and cook until the rice is nearly tender. Add the vegetables and water and simmer until they are cooked. (You may add more water if it is needed.) Season and serve.

This is an excellent side dish at a barbeque. You could also serve it with kebabs or steak at home or have two serves as a main meal.

Food units per serve
½ PR = pastrami
1 CB = rice
10 Optional Indulgences = oil

Seafood Salad

Serves 4
210 g (7 oz) salmon, drained, or any other seafood
1 egg, hardboiled and sliced
1 large continental cucumber, cut into quarters and finely sliced
1 small red onion, halved and sliced
3-4 large tomatoes, de-seeded and chopped
1 tablespoon parsley
2 cups cooked pasta, or 600 g (20 oz) potato, cooked and diced

Dressing
2 tablespoons light sour cream
1 tablespoon wholegrain mustard
2 teaspoons lemon juice
1 clove garlic, minced
125 ml (4 fl oz) low-fat unsweetened yoghurt
1 tablespoon capers, diced

1   Remove the skin and bones from the salmon.

2   Cut the cucumber into four sections and slice finely. Place all the salad
    ingredients except the egg into a bowl.

3   Combine all the dressing ingredients and mix well. Pour over the salad
    and mix through. Garnish with egg and serve.

For a different look, serve inside lettuce leaves or a tossed green salad.

Food units per serve.
1 PR = salmon, egg
1 CB = pasta
½ D = yoghurt
20 Optional Indulgences = sour cream

Shepherd's Pie

Serves 4

400 g (14 oz) beef or lamb, cubed
2 tablespoons flour
1 teaspoon olive oil
1 large onion, diced
125 ml (4 fl oz) red wine
125 ml (4 fl oz) boiling water
2 teaspoons beef stock powder
1 tablespoon Worcestershire sauce
2 tablespoons tomato paste
1 teaspoon prepared mustard
salt and freshly ground black pepper to taste
2 large sticks celery, sliced
3 large carrots, sliced
250 g (8 oz) mushrooms, sliced
600 g (20 oz) potato, peeled and diced
125 ml cup (4 fl oz) low-fat milk
50 g (2 oz) low-fat cheese, grated

1 Place the cubed meat and flour in a bag and shake until the meat is coated. Sauté the meat in the oil in a pan with the onion until browned. Add the red wine.

2 Mix the water, stock, Worcestershire sauce, tomato paste and seasoning together and gradually add to the meat.

3 Add the celery, carrots and mushrooms and simmer for one hour.

4 Boil the potatoes until tender. Drain and mash with milk then add the cheese.

5 Remove the meat mixture from the pan and place in an oven-proof dish. Spread the potato mixture over the top of the meat and rough the surface with a fork. Bake at 180°C for 20-25 minutes or until lightly browned. Serve with peas and green vegetables.

Food units per serve
2 PR = beef, cheese
1 CB = potato
1½ D = cheese
40 Optional Indulgences = flour, paste

Soy and Honey Warm Chicken Caesar Salad

Serves 4
1 tablespoon honey
3 tablespoons soy sauce
3 gloves garlic, minced
300 g (10 oz) chicken breast, cut into strips

Salad
cos lettuce
Lebanese cucumber, diced or sliced
tomatoes, diced
red onion, sliced
2 tablespoons bacon pieces
4 tablespoons parmesan cheese, grated
low-fat caesar dressing

1 Combine the honey, soy sauce and garlic. Marinate the chicken in this for at least 20 minutes.

2 Wash the cos lettuce and break or slice. Place it in a bowl and toss with the other vegetables. Sprinkle the bacon bits and cheese over the top. Add dressing according to your taste.

3 Sauté the chicken with the marinade in a non-stick pan until cooked. Scatter over the top of the salad and serve with crusty bread from your daily carbohydrate allowance.

> Vegetable quantities are entirely up to you as they are all free foods.

Food units per serve
2 PR = chicken, cheese
Optional Indulgences = check your brand of mayonnaise for the calorie count

Spaghetti with Bolognaise Sauce

Serves 2
1 onion, diced
2 cloves garlic, minced
200 g (7 oz) lean beef mince
410 g (14 oz) tinned diced tomatoes
410 g (14 oz) tinned crushed tomatoes
2 tablespoons tomato paste
125 ml (4 fl oz) cup red wine (optional)
125 ml (4 fl oz) water
1 teaspoon beef stock powder
250 g (8 oz) mushrooms, diced
1 teaspoon Italian mixed herbs
salt and freshly ground black pepper to taste
2 tablespoons parmesan cheese, shaved or grated
2 cups cooked spaghetti

1 Sauté the onion, garlic and mince in a non-stick pan until browned.

2 Add the undrained tomatoes, tomato paste, wine, water, stock, mushrooms, herbs and seasoning, and bring to the boil. Simmer for 25-35 minutes or until the sauce is thick and rich. Serve over cooked spaghetti and garnish with parmesan cheese.

Food units per serve
2 PR = mince
2 CB = pasta
50 Optional Indulgences = cheese, paste

Spring Rolls with Chilli Sauce

Serves 2
200 g (7 oz) chicken mince
2 cloves garlic, minced
1 onion, finely diced
250 g (8 oz) cabbage, shredded
1 large carrot, cut into matchsticks
2 teaspoons soy sauce
1 teaspoon cornflour
salt and freshly ground black pepper to taste
6 sheets filo pastry, cut in half
1 teaspoon sesame oil
sesame seeds to garnish

Chilli sauce
65 ml (2 fl oz) low-fat unsweetened yoghurt
1 tablespoon sweet chilli sauce

1 Combine all the ingredients for the spring rolls except the filo, oil and sesame seeds.

2 Divide the mixture into twelve equal portions. Take one sheet of filo and place a portion of the mixture at one end. Roll the filo over once, tuck in the sides, and continue to roll the filo and mixture until the end. This forms one spring roll. Repeat until you have made 12 rolls.

3 Brush the tops of the rolls with sesame oil and sprinkle with sesame seeds. Bake at 180°C for 25-30 minutes.

4 Combine the chilli sauce ingredients in a small bowl.

5 Serve the spring rolls with the chilli sauce and steamed green vegetables or a salad.

Food units per serve
2 PR = chicken
1 CB = filo
½ D = yoghurt
20 Optional Indulgences = cornflour, oil

Stir-fry Lamb on Rice

Serves 2
200 g (7 oz) lean lamb, thinly sliced
1 small onion, finely diced
1 teaspoon olive oil
1 packet French Onion soup mix
125 ml (4 oz) red wine
250 ml (8 fl oz) water
2 teaspoons cornflour
1 head of broccoli, lightly steamed
1 red capsicum, diced
1 whole bulb of garlic, roasted
2 cups cooked rice

1 Sauté the lamb and onion in the oil in a non-stick fry pan until the lamb
is just cooked. Combine the soup mix, red wine, water and cornflour then
add this to the pan. Stir until a sauce forms.

2 Add the broccoli and capsicum, and cook for a few minutes. (You may
add a little more water if it is needed.)

3 Squeeze out the garlic bulbs into the lamb and sauce. Serve immediately
on rice.

> To roast a garlic bulb, cut the very top off to expose the cloves. Wrap the bulbs in
> foil and bake until the garlic is soft enough to squeeze out.

Food units per serve
2 PR = lamb
2 CB = rice
40 Optional Indulgences = soup mix, cornflour

Stuffed Crispy Chicken with Chutney Sauce

Serves 1
100 g (3 oz) chicken breast
75 g (2½ oz) smooth low-fat cottage cheese
1 clove garlic, minced
1 tablespoon chives, diced
1 tablespoon low-fat unsweetened yoghurt
15 g cornflakes, crushed

Chutney sauce
1 tablespoon fruit chutney
65 ml (2 fl oz) low-fat unsweetened yoghurt

1 Carefully slit the chicken breasts across the middle, nearly to the other side (but do not cut them completely in half).

2 Mix the cheese, garlic and chives together. Stuff the chicken breasts with this mixture.

3 Roll the stuffed chicken breasts in yoghurt, then roll in the cornflakes.

4 Lightly spray an oven-proof dish with cooking spray and place the chicken breasts on the tray. Bake at 180°C for 25-30 minutes or until cooked through.

5 Combine the sauce ingredients. When the chicken is ready, pour the sauce over the breasts and serve with steamed vegetables.

Food units per serve
2 PR = chicken
½ CB = cornflakes
2 D = cheese
10 Optional Indulgences = yoghurt
2 D
or
90 Optional Indulgences = sauce

Stuffed Pita Pocket

Serves 1
1 medium pita bread
25 g (1 oz) low-fat cheese, grated
50 g (2 oz) ham
1 onion, diced finely
1 large tomato, diced

1 Split open the pita bread to form a pocket.

2 Fill with the ingredients and close.

3 Bake for 10-15 minutes on 180°C. Serve hot or cold with extra salad.

> Crushed pineapple can be added as well but goes a little soggy if left too long (1/2 cup = 1 fruit unit).

Food units used per serve
2 PR = ham, cheese
2 CB = pita

Stuffed Pizza Bread

Serves 8
2½ cups wholemeal self-raising flour
1 teaspoon baking powder
1 egg
125-250 ml (4-8 fl oz) light evaporated milk
2 tablespoons tomato paste
2 teaspoons Italian herbs
2 cloves garlic, minced
1 small onion, finely diced
100 g (4 oz) mushrooms, finely diced
½ red capsicum, finely diced
100 g (4 oz) ham, shredded
2 tablespoons parmesan cheese, grated

1   Preheat the oven to 200°C.

2   Put the flour and baking powder into a bowl and add the egg and half the evaporated milk. Stir to a firm dough. Add more milk if it is needed but make sure that the mixture is not too wet.

3   Roll the dough out then divide into two portions. Roll each portion out on a floured board until both portions are approximately 1 cm thick.

4   Combine the tomato paste, herbs and garlic and spread over one of the pizza bases. Top with the rest of the ingredients.

5   Place the second portion on top of the filling (like a sandwich). Brush the top of the pizza with milk or a little low-fat unsweetened yoghurt and bake for approximately 25-30 minutes or until cooked through. Season and serve.

> **This makes a delicious side dish with soup or salad.**

Food units per serve
½ PR = ham, cheese
1 CB = flour
½ D = milk
30 Optional Indulgences = tomato paste, flour

Super Open Sandwich

Serves 1
1 slice bread
1 tablespoon relish, cranberry sauce or mayonnaise
100 g (4 oz) chicken, turkey, ham or tinned fish
1-2 cups of salad vegetables (eg tomato, cucumber, grated carrot, lettuce, beetroot, bean sprouts)

1 Butter the bread with your choice of spread.

2 Place the meat on the bread and arrange the salad on top. Season and serve on a large plate. (You may need a knife and fork to eat this one!)

> This is a great way to enjoy a sandwich while only using one CB unit instead of two!

Food units used per serve
2 PR = meat
1 CB = bread
45 Optional Indulgences = relish

Sweet and Sour Meatballs

Serves 4
350 g (11 oz) lean mince
1 onion, finely diced
2 large carrots, grated finely
1 egg
2 cups cooked rice

Sauce
1 teaspoon chicken stock powder
65 ml (2 fl oz) white vinegar
4 teaspoons brown sugar
1 tablespoon cornflour
250 ml (8 fl oz) water
250 ml (8 fl oz) pineapple juice
2 tablespoons tomato paste
2 cups broccoli florets
1 large carrot, cut into matchsticks
100 g (4 oz) pineapple pieces

1 Combine the mince, onion, carrot and egg. Roll into balls then place on a greased oven-proof tray. Bake for 25 minutes at 180°C or until cooked.

2 Mix all the sauce ingredients except the broccoli, carrot and pineapple. Place in a pan and bring to the boil. Simmer for 10-15 minutes until thickened, then add the broccoli, carrot and pineapple. Cook until the vegetables are tender.

3 Remove the meat from the oven and place on top of boiled rice. Pour the sauce over the meat.

Food Units used per serve
2 PR = mince
1 CB = rice
$1/2$ F = pineapple juice and pieces
35 Optional Indulgences = tomato paste, sugar

Sweet Curry in a Hurry

Serves 4
1 teaspoon curry powder
400 g (14 oz) beef mince
1 large onion, diced
2 tablespoons fruit chutney
3 large carrots, diced or sliced
100 g (4 oz) peas
1 tablespoon flour
2 teaspoons chicken stock powder
500 ml (16 fl oz) water
250 g (8 oz) pineapple pieces
60 g (2 oz) sultanas
salt and freshly ground black pepper

1 Sauté the curry powder, mince and onion in a non-stick pan until browned. Add the chutney.

2 Add the carrots and peas.

3 Blend together the flour, stock and water. Add to the mince mixture and simmer until the carrots are tender.

4 Add the pineapple and sultanas and simmer for another 5 minutes. (You may add a little water if it is needed.) Season and serve over rice or as a filling inside a baked jacket potato from your carbohydrate allowance.

Food units per serve
2 PR = mince
1F = pineapple, sultanas
35 Optional Indulgences = chutney, flour

Tacos

Serves 4 (2 taco shells each serve)
200 g (7 oz) lean beef mince
1 large onion, diced
½ cup mushrooms, finely diced
¼ red capsicum, diced
¼ green capsicum, diced
200 g (7 oz) tinned Mexican chilli beans
chilli powder to taste
salt and freshly ground black pepper to taste
8 taco shells

Filling
shredded lettuce
sliced tomato
8 tablespoons low-fat cheese, grated
8 teaspoons light sour cream

1   Sauté the mince and onion in a non-stick pan until cooked. Add the mushrooms and capsicums and cook until tender.

2   Add the beans, chilli powder and seasonings. Stir until heated through.

3   Microwave the taco shells for 30 seconds (until pliable). Divide the bean mixture evenly between the shells.

4   Place 1 tablespoon cheese and 1 teaspoon sour cream on top of the meat. Add lettuce and tomato to taste and serve.

Although these are very tasty and easy meals, they can be quite messy to eat. They are not recommended for dinner guests!

Food units per serve (2 Tacos per serve)
2 PR = mince, beans, cheese
2 CB = taco shells
20 Optional Indulgences = sour cream

Texas Spuds

Serves 4
1 large onion, diced
100 g (4 oz) pastrami, diced
1 teaspoon olive oil
400 g (14 oz) tin baked beans in barbeque sauce
410 g (14 oz) tinned chopped tomatoes with herbs
2 cups vegetables (eg red capsicum, cauliflower, broccoli)
1 teaspoon dried thyme
4 x 300 g (10 oz) potatoes, baked in their jackets
50 g (2 oz) low-fat cheese, grated
2 tablespoons light sour cream

1 Sauté the onion and pastrami in the oil until the onion is almost cooked.

2 Add the beans, tomatoes, vegetables and thyme and simmer until the mixture thickens.

3 Heat the baked potatoes and split them open. Place equal quantities of bean mixture over each potato. Sprinkle a little cheese over the mixture and top with sour cream. Serve with plenty of salad.

Food units per serve
2 PR = pastrami, cheese, beans
2 CB = potato
25 Optional Indulgences = sour cream, oil

Thai Fish in Red Sauce

Serves 2
1 onion, sliced
2 large carrots, sliced thinly
1 tablespoon white wine
410 g (14 oz) tinned chopped tomatoes
1 teaspoon Thai red curry paste
1 tablespoon fish sauce
250 g (8 oz) white fish fillets or prawns
65 ml (2 fl oz) low-fat unsweetened yoghurt
1 tablespoon light sour cream
½ teaspoon coconut essence
1 tablespoon fresh coriander

1 Cook the onions and carrots in wine for 2 minutes.

2 Add the tomatoes, curry paste and fish sauce, then bring to the boil. Add the fish, reduce the heat and simmer for 5 minutes or until the fish is cooked.

3 Combine the yoghurt, sour cream and coconut essence. Stir through the tomato and fish mixture. Add the coriander and serve immediately over rice from your carbohydrate allowance.

Food units used per serve
2 PR = fish
½ D = yoghurt
15 Optional Indulgences = sour cream

Tomato and Coriander Salsa

½ red capsicum, roasted and finely diced
4 large tomatoes, finely diced
1 bunch spring onions, finely sliced
1 cucumber, seeds removed and diced
2 limes, juiced
2 green chillies
2 tablespoons coriander leaves
salt and freshly ground black pepper to taste

1 Mix all the vegetables in a bowl. Add the lime juice and salt and pepper.

2 Wash the coriander leaves and chop finely, removing excess stems. Add to the vegetables.

3 Wash the chillies, cut in half and de-seed. Chop the chillies finely and add to the vegetables. Serve.

> For a different taste, you can vary the amount of chilli or add garlic.
>
> To roast capsicum, cut into large chunks and place under the grill until the skin bubbles. Remove, cool and peel.
>
> To de-seed the cucumber, cut into four lengthways and run a sharp knife down the centre to remove the seeds.

Food units used per serve
0

Tomato and Parmesan Risotto

Serves 4

1 large onion, diced
2 cloves garlic, minced
1 cup arborio rice
1 teaspoon olive oil
½ cup (4 fl oz) dry white wine
2 cups boiling water
2 teaspoons chicken stock powder
400 g (14 oz) mushrooms, sliced
820 g (28 oz) tinned diced tomatoes
2 tablespoons basil, shredded
1 tablespoon light sour cream
8 tablespoons parmesan cheese, shaved or grated
salt and freshly ground black pepper to taste

1 Sauté the onion and garlic in the oil until soft. Add the rice and stir until covered in oil.

2 Combine the boiling water and stock powder and add to the rice. Add the wine.

3 Simmer, stirring occasionally, until all the liquid is absorbed and the rice is tender.

4 Add the mushrooms and tomatoes and cook for 5 minutes. Add the basil, sour cream and cheese and stir through. Season and serve with a green salad.

Food units per serve
1 PR = cheese
1 CB = rice
20 Optional Indulgences = oil, sour cream

Tropical Wild Rice Salad

Serves 4
½ cup wild rice
½ cup long grain rice
100 g (4 oz) pineapple pieces
1 cup fresh or tinned mango, diced
30 g (1 oz) dried apricots, diced
1 red capsicum, diced
4 large sticks celery, finely sliced
2 tablespoons fresh mint, chopped

Dressing
1 tablespoon macadamia oil
1 tablespoon balsamic vinegar
salt and freshly ground black pepper to taste

1   Cook the rices separately as the wild rice takes approximately 40 minutes to cook. Drain and rinse well.

2   Combine the dressing ingredients.

3   Mix all the remaining ingredients together in a bowl. Pour the dressing over, chill and serve.

Food units per serve
1 CB = rice
1 F = fruits
45 Optional Indulgences = oil

Tuna and Celery Risotto

Serves 2
1 large onion, sliced
2 cloves garlic, minced
1 teaspoon butter
1 cup arborio rice
125 ml (4 fl oz) dry white wine
750 ml boiling water
2 teaspoons chicken stock powder
4 large sticks celery, cut in half and sliced
1 teaspoon dried oregano
1 tablespoon lemon rind
4 tablespoons parmesan cheese, grated
100 g (4 oz) tuna in brine, drained
1 tablespoon light sour cream
freshly ground black pepper

1 Sauté the onion and garlic in the butter for a few minutes. Add the rice and stir to cover the rice in butter.

2 Add the wine, boiling water and stock and cook until the rice is tender. (You may add a little more water if needed.) Add the celery, oregano and lemon rind and cook for 2-3 minutes, stirring constantly. Add the cheese and sour cream. Lastly add the tuna and heat through. Serve.

Food units per serve
2 PR = tuna, cheese
2 CB = rice
35 Optional Indulgences = butter, sour cream

Tuna and Tomato Parcels

Serves 4
185 g (6 oz) tin tuna, drained
2 large de-seeded tomatoes, diced
3 large sticks celery, finely sliced
4 spring onions, finely sliced
75 g (2½ oz) low-fat cheese, grated
1 tablespoon lemon rind
1 tablespoon lemon juice
1 tablespoon fresh basil
2 tablespoons light sour cream
125 ml (4 fl oz) low-fat unsweetened yoghurt
1 teaspoon cornflour
1 cup cooked rice
12 sheets filo pastry
sesame or poppy seeds to taste

1 Combine all the ingredients except the filo pastry and seeds.

2 Take three sheets of filo and place each sheet on top of the other. Divide the mixture into four and place a portion at one end of the filo. Roll over once, then tuck in the sides and continue rolling to the end. Repeat to make four parcels.

3 Lightly spray an oven tray with cooking spray. Place the parcels on the tray, spray the tops with cooking spray and sprinkle with sesame seeds or poppy seeds. Bake at 180ºC for 30 minutes. Serve with a salad and lemon wedges.

> This recipe works just as well with tinned salmon. Freeze when cooked and reheat in the oven to crisp up.

Food units per serve
2 PR = tuna, cheese
1½ CB = filo, rice
½ D = yoghurt
25 Optional Indulgences = cornflour, sour cream

Tuna Quiche

Serves 4
1 cup self-raising flour
375 ml (12 fl oz) low-fat milk
4 eggs
300 g (10 oz) tuna in brine or water, drained
2 large zucchini, grated and squeezed
2 large carrots, grated
1 cup corn kernels
1 onion, diced
zest and juice of ½ lemon
salt and freshly ground black pepper to taste
75 g (2½ oz) low-fat cheese, grated

1 Combine the flour, milk and eggs together with a whisk.

2 Mix and add the remaining ingredients, except the cheese. Spray a large quiche dish with cooking spray or oil lightly and pour in the mixture. Sprinkle the cheese over the top.

3 Bake at 200°C for approximately 45 minutes or until set. Serve hot or cold.

> Zucchini can have a lot of juice. If you have time, you can grate and sprinkle with salt then let it sit for 20 minutes. Otherwise, grate the zucchini and squeeze once to remove the juice. If you don't remove the excess juice, the quiche can take longer to cook.

Food units used per serve
2 PR = egg, tuna
1 CB = flour, corn
1½ D = milk, cheese

Turkey and Cranberry Sub

Serves 1
60-80 g (2-3 oz) long crusty bread roll
50 g (2 oz) turkey, shaved
1 tablespoon cranberry sauce
25 g (1 oz) mozzarella cheese
2 leaves lettuce, shredded
1 tomato, thickly sliced
alfalfa sprouts

1 Slice the roll in half. On the bottom half spread the cranberry sauce, and add the turkey and cheese. Place under the grill until the cheese bubbles.

2 Toast the other half of the roll at the same time. Remove and fill with the lettuce, tomato and sprouts. Serve.

This is a tasty quick and easy lunch recipe.
If you cannot toast the roll, then just eat it as a sandwich.

Food units per serve
1 PR = turkey, cheese
2 CB = roll
2 D = cheese
20 Optional Indulgences = cranberry

Veal Cannelloni

Serves 2
200 g (7 oz) veal, minced
1 onion, finely diced
1 teaspoon olive oil
2 cups mushrooms, finely diced
1 teaspoon dried Italian herbs
125 ml (4 fl oz) tomato juice
salt and freshly ground black pepper to taste
12 cannelloni tubes
1 zucchini, diced
410 g (14 oz) tinned tomatoes
125 ml (4 fl oz) low-fat unsweetened yoghurt
1 egg
25 g (1 oz) low-fat cheese
1 teaspoon prepared mustard

1 Sauté the veal and onion in oil until browned. Add the mushrooms, herbs and seasonings. Cook for 2-3 minutes, then remove from the heat. Add the tomato juice and cool.

2 Fill the cannelloni tubes with equal quantities of the mixture and lay the tubes in the bottom of an oven-proof dish sprayed with cooking spray.

3 Combine the zucchini and tomatoes and pour over the tubes.

4 Combine the yoghurt, egg, cheese and mustard and pour over the tomato mixture. Bake at 180°C for approximately 40 minutes. Serve.

Food units per serve
2 PR = veal mince
2 CB = cannelloni
2 D = yoghurt, cheese
40 Optional Indulgences = egg, oil

Vegie Patties with Satay Sauce

Serves 4
2 cups uncooked red lentils
½ cup long-grain white rice
½ cup brown rice
2 slices multi-grain or wholemeal bread, crumbed
1 onion, finely diced
2 cups pumpkin, grated
2 large carrots, grated
3 spring onions, thinly sliced
1 tablespoon sweet chilli sauce or chilli powder to taste
salt and freshly ground black pepper to taste

Sauce
125 ml (4 fl oz) low-fat unsweetened yoghurt
1½ tablespoons peanut butter, crunchy
1 tablespoon sweet chilli sauce

1. Add the lentils to a pan of boiling water and simmer uncovered about 5 minutes or until tender. Drain (do not rinse).

2. Cook the rices separately, then drain (do not rinse). Process the lentils and rices together until combined. Refrigerate the mixture until it thickens.

3. Add the breadcrumbs, vegetables, chilli and seasonings. Mix well until a sticky mixture is formed and then divide into four portions. Shape the portions into patties of the desired size. Bake at 180°C for approximately 30-40 minutes.

4. Combine the sauce ingredients together and serve over the patties.

This satay sauce is also delicious over kebabs or a chicken breast.

Food units per serve
2 PR = lentils
1½ CB = rice, bread
Sauce
½ D and 50 Optional Indulgences, or 75 Optional Indulgences

Vegetable Flan

Serves 6

½ cup self-raising flour
5 eggs, beaten
1 onion, diced
1 zucchini, grated
1 large carrot, grated
1 red capsicum, diced
2 spring onions, sliced
1 cup mushrooms, diced
100 g (4 oz) frozen peas
½ cup frozen corn
250 g (8 oz) cottage cheese
250 ml (8 fl oz) low-fat unsweetened yoghurt
6 tablespoons parmesan cheese, grated
salt and freshly ground black pepper to taste

1 Combine the ingredients and pour into a large quiche dish sprayed with cooking spray.

2 Bake at 160ºC for one hour or until set. Serve hot or cold with a green salad.

Food units per serve
2 PR = eggs, cheese
1 D = yoghurt
½ CB = flour, corn

Vegetable Frittata

Serves 1
1 onion, diced
2 cups grated vegetables (eg zucchini, carrot, pumpkin)
100 g sweet potato, diced small
1 teaspoon olive oil
2 eggs, beaten
salt and freshly ground black pepper to taste

1 Sauté all the vegetables in the oil until tender In a non-stick pan.

2 Pour over the egg and season. Cook until set. Serve.

> You may like to pop the mixture under the grill to brown the top.

Food units per serve
2 PR = eggs
1 CB = potato
45 Optional Indulgences = oil

Vegetarian Lasagne

Serves 4
1 large onion, diced
2 cloves garlic, minced
1 teaspoon olive oil
820 g (27 oz) tinned diced tomatoes
2 tablespoons tomato paste
65 ml (2 fl oz) water
2 tablespoons parsley
250 g (8 oz) frozen spinach, thawed and well-drained
160 g (5½ oz) ricotta cheese
½ teaspoon nutmeg
375 ml (12 fl oz) light evaporated milk
1 tablespoon cornflour
250 g (8 oz) mushrooms, sliced
salt and freshly ground black pepper to taste
250 g (8 oz) pre-cooked lasagne sheets
100 g (4 oz) low-fat cheese, grated

1 Sauté the onion and garlic in the oil for 2 minutes. Add the undrained tomatoes, tomato paste and water and bring to the boil. Simmer for 5 minutes. Stir in the parsley and set aside.

2 Combine the spinach, ricotta cheese and nutmeg in a bowl. Add ½ cup evaporated milk and stir through.

3 Combine the remaining evaporated milk and cornflour. Bring to the boil, stirring constantly, until thickened. Add the mushrooms and simmer for 2 minutes, then add salt and pepper and remove from the heat.

4 Spray an oven-proof dish with cooking spray. Place one layer of lasagne sheets on the base of a dish and spread over half the tomato mixture. Add another layer of sheets and spread over the spinach mixture. Add a third layer of sheets and spread over mushroom mixture. Add a final layer of sheets and spread the remaining tomato mixture on top.

5 Sprinkle with the cheese and bake at 180ºC for approximately 50 minutes. Serve hot or cold with a green salad.

Food units per serve
2 PR = cheeses
2 CB = lasagne
1½ D = milk
25 Optional Indulgences = cornflour, oil, tomato paste

Warm Lamb Salad

Serves 2
200 g (7 oz) lamb, cut into strips
1 teaspoon olive oil
salad vegetables (eg cucumber, tomato, capsicum)
lettuce

Mint dressing
1 teaspoon olive oil
2 teaspoons balsamic vinegar
1 tablespoon tomato juice
2 teaspoons water
2 cloves garlic, minced
1 tablespoon fresh mint, finely chopped
salt and freshly ground black pepper to taste

1 Sauté the lamb in the oil until cooked but still pink.

2 Combine the dressing ingredients in a screw-top container. Shake well and chill.

3 Arrange the lettuce and salad ingredients in a bowl. Add the lamb and pour over the dressing. Serve with a crusty bread roll from your carbohydrate allowance.

Food units per serve
2 PR = lamb
45 Optional Indulgences = oil

Wholegrain Vegetable Parcels

Serves 4
250 ml low-fat unsweetened yoghurt
1 tablespoon cornflour
1-2 teaspoons wholegrain mustard
salt and freshly ground black pepper to taste
100 g (4 oz) low-fat cheese, grated
1 red capsicum, diced
1 large onion, diced
2-3 large zucchini
2 cups cauliflower, cut into small florets
12 sheets filo pastry

1 Mix the yoghurt, cornflour, mustard and seasonings. Add the cheese and vegetables and stir until vegetables are covered.

2 Take three sheets of filo and place each sheet on top of the other. Divide the vegetable mixture into four and place one portion on the filo sheets. Roll the filo over once, tuck in the sides and roll to the end. Place on a cooking tray with cooking spray. Repeat this process until you have four parcels.

3 Spray the tops of the parcels with cooking spray and sprinkle sesame or poppy seeds over the top. Bake at 180°C for 30-40 minutes. Serve with a salad or Baked Vegetables (page 77).

These parcels can be frozen when cooked and reheated in the oven to crisp up.

Food units per serve
1 PR = cheese
1 CB = filo
1 D = yoghurt
10 Optional Indulgences = cornflour

Desserts

Apple and Blueberry Filo Pies

Serves 4
½ cup frozen blueberries
1 teaspoon orange zest
2 teaspoons brown sugar
4 large apples, peeled and cored
8–12 sheets filo pastry

1   Combine the blueberries, zest and sugar. Stuff the mix evenly into the cored apples. Place each apple in the centre of 2–3 filo sheets and pull the sheets around. Press the edges of the sheets together at the top, so as to look like a bag. Repeat with the other 3 apples.

2   Place in an oven-proof dish and bake at 180°C for 25–30 minutes or until the apple is soft.

> If you have spare Optional Indulgences you could serve this with low-fat icecream.

Food units per serve
1 CB = filo
1 F = apple
20 Optional Indulgences = blueberries, sugar

Apricot Slice with Lemon Glaze

Serves 8

4 tablespoons butter
2 teaspoons honey
½ cup rolled oats
¼ cup self-raising wholemeal flour
5 teaspoons artificial sweetener
25 g (1 oz) coconut
½ cup tinned apricot, drained and diced

Icing

8 teaspoons icing sugar
1 teaspoon butter
1 teaspoon boiling water
1 teaspoon lemon zest
1 teaspoon lemon juice

1 Preheat the oven to 180°C.

2 Melt the butter and honey together in a microwave or small pot. Mix the dry ingredients together. Add the melted butter and honey to the dry ingredients and mix well. Add the apricots and mix through.

3 Spray a baking tin (loaf size is best) with cooking spray. Press the apricot mixture into the tin and bake at 180°C for 30-35 minutes.

4 Combine the icing sugar, butter and hot water and mix well. Add the lemon zest and juice. Ice the apricot slice when warm or cold.

> This dish is very tasty, so be careful not to over-indulge!

Food units per serve
140 Optional Indulgences or 1 CB and 40 Optional Indulgences

Baked Apricot Cheesecake

Serves 6
250 g (8 oz) low-fat smooth cottage cheese
juice and rind of ½ lemon
juice of ½ orange
2 tablespoons artificial sweetener
1 tablespoon light sour cream
1 tablespoon custard powder
1 egg yolk
2 egg whites
2 teaspoons caster sugar
400 g (14 oz) tinned pie apricots, drained

1 Blend the cheese, lemon juice and rind, orange juice, sweetener, sour cream, custard powder and egg yolk together.

2 Beat the egg whites until stiff then add the caster sugar and beat until dissolved.

3 Fold the egg white mixture into the cheese mixture.

4 Place the apricots on the base of an oven-proof dish and cover with the mixture. Bake at 180ºC for approximately 30 minutes or until firm. Cool and serve.

> The longer this cheesecake is left the better it gets. This is a refreshing substitute for trifle and cream. Try experimenting with other fruits.

Food units per serve
1 D = cottage cheese
½ F = apricots
35 Optional Indulgences = egg, custard powder, sour cream, sugar

Banana and Blueberry Muffins

Serves 10

1 cup self-raising wholemeal flour
1 cup plain flour
4 teaspoons artificial sweetener
½ teaspoon bicarbonate of soda
½ teaspoon mixed spice
½ teaspoon ground cinnamon
2 tablespoons golden syrup
1 ripe banana, mashed
375 ml (13 fl oz) buttermilk
1½ cups blueberries

1   Preheat the oven to 180ºC.

2   Sift the flours into a bowl. Add the sweetener, bicarbonate of soda and spices.

3   In another bowl combine the golden syrup, mashed banana and buttermilk. Add the buttermilk mixture to the flour mixture and stir until just combined. Fold in the blueberries.

4   Spray 10 muffin moulds with cooking spray and fill with the mixture. Bake at 180ºC for approximately 20 minutes or until the tops are lightly golden. Allow to cool.

Food units per serve
Each muffin = 130 Optional Indulgences or 1 CB and 30 Optional Indulgences

Banana Smoothie

Serves 1
1 ripe banana, frozen
250 ml (8 fl oz) low-fat milk
1 teaspoon honey
1 teaspoon vanilla essence

1 Place all the ingredients into a blender.

2 Blend until smooth.

This is a great way to use up ripened bananas. Bananas can be frozen if you first remove the skin and wrap in plastic wrap.

Food units per serve
1 F = banana
2 D = milk
15 Optional Indulgences = honey

Berry Nice Scones

Serves 8
2 cups self-raising flour
pinch salt
200 ml (7 fl oz) tub low-fat berry yoghurt
65–125 ml (2–4 fl oz) diet lemonade

1 Preheat the oven to 200°C.

2 Place the dry ingredients in a bowl. Fold the yoghurt through then add the lemonade gradually to form a firm dough. (A sticky dough is harder to cook, so you should use just enough lemonade to make a firm dough.)

3 Turn the dough out onto a lightly floured board. Roll or press to make 8 scones. Lightly spray a baking tray with cooking spray. Place the scones on the tray and bake at 200°C for approximately 10 minutes or until golden.

> Serve with diet or 100 per cent fruit jam of choice, dairy whip cream out of your Optional Indulgences, or 80 g ricotta cheese mixed with 2 tablespoons jam. Each tablespoon of the cheese and jam mixture will use up 20 Optional Indulgence calories.

Food units per serve
1 CB = flours
½ D = yoghurt

Bread and Rice Pudding

Serves 4
400 g (14 oz) tinned pie apples or fruit of your choice, drained
30 g (1 oz) sultanas
1 cup cooked short or medium grain rice
500 ml (18 fl oz) low-fat milk
1 egg
½ teaspoon mixed spice
½ teaspoon cinnamon
1 teaspoon vanilla essence
2 tablespoons 100 per cent fruit or diet jam
2 slices fruit or raisin bread

1   Place the apples over the base of an oven-proof dish, sprinkle with the sultanas and spread the rice over the top.

2   Beat the milk, egg, spices and vanilla together.

3   Spread the jam over the bread then cut the bread into small bite-size pieces. Sprinkle the bread over the rice. Pour the milk mix over the bread and stand for 15-20 minutes.

4   Bake at 180ºC for approximately 40-50 minutes or until set. Remove from the oven and allow to cool for 10 minutes. Serve alone or with cream or icecream from your Optional Indulgences.

> This is a very filling dish that can be eaten anytime of the day.

Food units per serve
2 CB = rice, bread
1 F = apples, sultanas
2 D = milk
20 Optional Indulgences = egg

Brown Honey Scones

Serves 12
1½ cups wholemeal self-raising flour
1 teaspoon baking powder
pinch of salt
1 tablespoon butter
125 ml (4 fl oz) low-fat milk
1½ tablespoons honey
60 g (2 oz) sultanas

1 Combine the flour, baking powder and salt. Rub in the butter.

2 Warm the milk (be careful not to boil) then dissolve the honey in it. Add it to the flour mixture and mix into a soft dough. (You may add a little more milk if it is necessary.) Turn the dough out onto a lightly floured board and divide into 12 portions. Lightly spray a baking tray with cooking spray. Pleace scones on the tray and bake for 10-15 minutes in a hot oven. Serve with diet or 100% fruit jam.

Food units per serve
½ CB = flour
45 Optional Indulgences = honey, milk, butter

Chocolate Banana Parcels

Serves 1
1 sheet filo pastry
1 banana
8 chocolate buttons (10 g or ⅓ oz)

1 Cut the sheet of filo in half.

2 Cut the banana in half. Place 4 buttons across one end of the filo then place the banana on top of the buttons. Fold the sides of the filo over the banana to the centre, roll once, then tuck in the sides. Roll the filo sheet into a parcel. Repeat to make a second parcel.

3 Spray the top of the parcels with cooking spray and bake at 180°C for 20 minutes or until browned.

> **This is lovely served with Irish Cream Custard (page 193).**

Food units per serve
1F = banana
100 Optional Indulgences = filo, buttons

Chocolate Mousse

Serves 4

250 ml (8 fl oz) low-fat unsweetened yoghurt or 200 ml (7 fl oz) flavoured diet yoghurt

250 g (8 oz) smooth cottage cheese

2 tablespoons light sour cream

2 ripe bananas, mashed or 1 cup pears, mashed

3 teaspoons gelatine

125 ml (4 fl oz) boiling water

2¹/₂ tablespoons low-fat chocolate drink powder

1 Blend the yoghurt, cottage cheese, sour cream and mashed banana or pears together.

2 Dissolve the gelatine in boiling water. Add the chocolate drink powder and stir. Pour into the blender and blend until smooth.

3 Pour into 4 parfait glasses and refrigerate until set.

This is not only a wonderful treat for those who love chocolate, but is also an impressive dessert for guests, who will never believe it is from a weight loss book!

Food units per serve

170 Optional Indulgences

or

¹/₂ F = banana or pear

2 D = cheese, yoghurt

40 Optional Indulgences = sour cream, chocolate mix

Chocolate Self-saucing Pudding

Serves 6
2 tablespoons butter
2 teaspoons cocoa
8 teaspoons artificial sweetener
1¼ cup self-raising flour
1 teaspoon baking powder
250 ml (8 fl oz) low-fat milk
1 teaspoon vanilla essence
400 g (14 oz) tinned pie fruit of your choice, drained

Chocolate Sauce
4 teaspoons soft brown sugar
2 teaspoons cocoa
310 ml (10 fl oz) boiling water

1 Pre-heat the oven to 180°C.

2 Melt the butter then stir in the cocoa and sweetener. Add the milk and vanilla essence and gently whisk together.

3 Add the sifted flour and baking powder and gently whisk into a batter.

4 Place the fruit at the bottom of an oven-proof dish and pour over the batter mixture.

5 Mix the brown sugar and cocoa together, then sprinkle over the top of the batter mixture. Gently pour over the boiling water. (This looks terrible but don't worry – it will work beautifully!) Bake at 180°C for 30-35 minutes. Serve.

Food units per serve
160 Optional Indulgences
or
½ CB = flour
½ F = tinned pie fruit
70 Optional Indulgences = cocoa, butter, sugar

Cream Cheese Sponge Roll

Serves 8
10 teaspoons brown sugar
3 eggs
artificial sweetener to taste (I find this sweet enough without it)
2 ripe bananas, mashed
1 cup self-raising flour
2 teaspoons ground ginger
160 g (5½ oz) light cream cheese
6 teaspoons golden syrup
½ teaspoon vanilla essence

1 Beat the brown sugar, eggs and sweetener together until light and frothy. Add the mashed bananas and beat through. Sift in the flour and ginger and stir through with a fork until combined.

2 Spray a non-stick sponge roll tin with cooking spray. Spread the mixture in the tin. Bake at 180ºC for approximately 15 minutes or until the centre of the cake springs back when touched lightly. Loosen the edges with a knife, then invert the cake onto a clean tea towel. Roll up and leave to cool.

3 Beat the cream cheese, golden syrup and vanilla together.

4 Unroll the cake when it is almost cool and spread with the cream cheese mixture. Roll up again and cut into 8 slices.

Food units per serve
160 Optional Indulgences
or
½ F = banana
½ PR = eggs
½ CB = flour
50 Optional Indulgences = cheese, sugar, syrup

Custard

Serves 2
250 ml (8 fl oz) low-fat milk
1 tablespoon custard powder
2 teaspoons sugar
2 teaspoons hot water
dash vanilla essence

1   Place custard powder, vanilla essence and water together in a small saucepan. Stir together until mixture has a smooth consistency.

2   Add milk to saucepan and simmer over low heat, stirring. When mixture is hot (don't let it boil) and thicker, remove from heat and allow to sit for a minute to thicken. Serve.

Food units per serve
1 D = milk
25 Optional Indulgences = custard powder, sugar, vanilla essence

Fruit Turnover

Serves 1
1 cup cooked or tinned fruit, drained
cinnamon to taste
2 teaspoons brown sugar (optional)
3 sheets filo pastry

1 Place 3 sheets of filo on top of each other. At one end sprinkle the brown sugar. Place the fruit on top of the sugar and sprinkle with cinnamon.

2 Roll over once, tuck in the sides and finish rolling up. Lightly spray a baking tray with cooking spray. Place turnovers onto tray. Spray the top of the parcel with cooking spray and bake for 15 minutes at 180°C until brown.

Food units used per serve
1 CB = filo
2F = fruit
30 Optional Indulgences = sugar

Fruity Icecream

Serves 1
1 ripe banana, frozen
65 ml (2 fl oz) low-fat milk

1 Place the ingredients in a blender and blend until thick and creamy. (You may add a little milk if it is needed).

2 Freeze until firm.

> You can substitute other frozen fruits for the banana. Try using mango, rockmelon or paw paw.

Food units used per serve
1 F = banana
½ D = milk

Fruity Nut Loaf

Serves 6

30 g (1 oz) sultanas
1 egg, lightly beaten
1 tablespoon macadamia nut oil (or peanut oil)
1 tablespoon golden syrup
2 large carrots, grated
1 banana, mashed
½ cup pineapple, crushed
1½ cups wholemeal self-raising flour
1 teaspoon cinnamon
1 teaspoon baking soda
½ cup bran flakes
60 g (2 oz) pecans or walnuts, chopped

1 Cover the sultanas in boiling water and soak for at least 30 minutes.

2 Beat the egg, oil and golden syrup together. Add the carrot, banana and pineapple.

3 Sift the flour, cinnamon and baking soda together. Place the husks from the flour back into the mixture. Add the bran and stir through.

4 Add the pecans and drained sultanas and stir through. Spray a loaf tin (or cake tin if you prefer) with cooking spray and fill with the mixture. Bake at 160°C for approximately 1½ hours or until cooked.

> This is a nice moist loaf. For a Christmas treat, you could add some brandy.

Food units per serve
1 PR = nuts, egg
1 CB = flour
1 F = sultana, pineapple, banana
35 Optional Indulgences = bran, oil, golden syrup

Irish Cream Custard

Serves 6
250 ml (4 fl oz) cup low-fat milk
1 tablespoon custard powder
1 tablespoon Irish Cream liqueur
artificial sweetener to taste

1   Combine the custard powder and milk together and heat until thickened, stirring to prevent burning and lumps. (Alternatively you could microwave for 1 minute.) Remove from the heat and stir the Irish Cream through the mixture.

2   Taste and adjust the sweetness by adding sweetener to taste.

Food units per serve
40 Optional Indulgences = custard power, milk, Irish Cream liqueur

Jelly Whip

Serves 1
185 g (3 oz) diet jelly
250 ml (8 fl oz) boiling water
250 ml (8 fl oz) low-fat unsweetened yoghurt or 200 ml (7 fl oz) flavoured
diet yoghurt

1 Dissolve the jelly in water and set aside to cool for 10 minutes.

2 Add the yoghurt and beat together until fluffy. Set in the refrigerator.

You can add fruit to the jelly before leaving to set.

Food units per serve
2 D = yoghurt or 80 Optional Indulgences

Meringue Rice Pudding

Serves 4
1 cup white short or medium grain rice
375 ml (12 fl oz) water
500 g (16 fl oz) low-fat milk
2 eggs, separated
1 teaspoon vanilla essence
2 teaspoons artificial sweetener
2 teaspoons castor sugar
400 g (14 oz) tinned pie fruit, drained

1 Simmer the rice in water until the water is absorbed. Add the milk and simmer until the rice is cooked.

2 Beat the egg yolks, vanilla and sweetener together. Stir into the rice mixture.

3 Beat the egg whites until stiff. Add the castor sugar and beat until very stiff and glossy.

4 Place the fruit in a pie dish or 4 individual dishes. Place the rice on top of the fruit, then the egg whites on top of the rice.

5 Bake at 180°C for 20 minutes or until the meringue is golden brown.

Food units used per serve
1 CB = rice
1 F = fruit
2 D = milk
½ PR = egg
10 Optional Indulgences = castor sugar

Mint Choc Chip Mud Pie

Serves 6

8 chocolate wheaten biscuits
2 ripe bananas, mashed
250 g (8 oz) tub smooth cottage cheese
250 ml (8 fl oz) low-fat unsweetened yoghurt
1 tablespoon brown sugar
2 tablespoons light sour cream
1 teaspoon peppermint essence
4 teaspoons gelatine
125 ml (4 fl oz) boiling water
2½ tablespoons low-fat mint chocolate drink powder

1   Crush the biscuits roughly (so there are still some chunky pieces) and sprinkle over the base of a pie dish (no nibbling!).

2   Blend the banana, cottage cheese, yoghurt, sugar, light sour cream and essence in a blender.

3   Dissolve the gelatine in boiling water. Add the mint chocolate drink powder and stir until dissolved. Add this to the cottage cheese mixture and blend.

4   Pour over the biscuits. (They will start to float.) Place in the refrigerator and leave for approximately 1½ hours or until set.

> **This is great when you need a chocolate fix!**

Food units per serve
½ D = cheese, yoghurt
½ F = banana
180 Optional Indulgences = biscuits, sour cream, sugar, mint chocolate drink powder

Orange and Mango Cheesecake

Serves 4-6
12 arrowroot biscuits
1 teaspoon butter, melted
2 teaspoons boiling water
250 ml (8 fl oz) boiling water
185 g (3 oz) diet jelly, orange
125 ml (4 fl oz) boiling water
185 g (3 oz) diet jelly, mango
3 teaspoons gelatine
250 g (8 oz) low-fat smooth cottage cheese
4 cups cold pumpkin, cooked and mashed
250 ml (8 fl oz) low-fat unsweetened yoghurt
2 tablespoons dairy whip cream
2 teaspoons ground ginger
4 teaspoons brown sugar
250 ml (8 fl oz) diet ginger ale

1   Crush the biscuits in a plastic bag. Place in a bowl with the melted butter and add 2 teaspoons of boiling water to the biscuits to help bind them. (It should be moist enough for the crumbs to stick together.) Spray a pie dish with cooking spray and press the crumbs on the base. Place in the freezer.

2   Add the cup of boiling water to one of the jelly sachets, add the gelatine and stir until dissolved.

3   Combine the cottage cheese, pumpkin, yoghurt, cream, ginger and sugar and blend well. Add the jelly mixture and ginger ale, then pour over the biscuit base. Chill in the refrigerator until set.

4   Add 125 ml (4 fl oz) boiling water to the second jelly sachet. Allow to cool but not set. Pour over the top of the set cheesecake and refrigerate until the jelly is set.

> If you can't find arrowroot biscuits, you can use any biscuit with a calorie count of approximately 36 calories per biscuit.

Food units per serve
4 serves: 1 PR = cottage cheese
          1 CB = biscuits
          1 D = yoghurt
25 Optional Indulgences = sugar, cream
6 serves: 180 optional indulgences

Pancake Jack-a-Stack

Serves 1
½ cup self-raising flour
½ cup (4 fl oz) low-fat milk
1 egg
1 banana, mashed

1 Combine the flour, milk and egg together with a whisk. Mix through the banana.

2 Grease a non-stick pan and place spoonfuls of the batter into the pan. Cook until bubbles form on top then turn over. Serve.

Try experimenting with other fruits. Grated apple and cinnamon also taste delicious.

This dish can be served for breakfast, or morning or afternoon teas. If you wish, you could add maple syrup from your Optional Indulgences.

Food units used per serve
1 PR = egg
2 CB = flour
1 F = banana
1 D = milk

Peach Muffins

Serves 12
30 g (1 oz) sultanas
250 ml (8 fl oz) boiling water
1 cup self-raising wholemeal flour
1 cup self-raising plain flour
1 teaspoon mixed spice
1 tablespoon cocoa
2 eggs
2 bananas, mashed
400 g tinned pie peaches, drained
2 teaspoons vanilla essence
3 teaspoons artificial sweetener

1 Soak the sultanas in boiling water for at least 30 minutes.

2 Sift the flours, spice and cocoa together. Return the wholemeal husks to the mix after sifting. Make a well in the middle of the dry ingredients.

3 Place the eggs, bananas, peaches, sultanas and water, vanilla and sweetener into the well. Mix through quickly and thoroughly with a fork.

4 Spray 12 standard muffin tins or 36 small muffin tins with cooking spray and fill with the mixture. Bake at 160°C for approximately 40 minutes.

Food units per serve (1 large muffin or 3 small)
½ CB = flours
½ F = sultana, peach, banana
35 Optional Indulgences = eggs, cocoa, some flour

Peachy Pancakes

Serves 1
½ cup self-raising flour (white or wholemeal)
125 ml (4 fl oz) low-fat milk
1 egg
½ cup peaches, tinned and drained or fresh
1 teaspoon lemon zest

1 Combine flour, milk and egg together with a whisk. Cut peaches into small pieces. Add peaches and lemon zest to egg mixture and stir through.

2 Lightly spray a non-stick pan with cooking spray and place the mixture in the pan in large spoonfuls. Cook until bubbles form on the top, then turn over. Serve stacked with maple syrup from your Optional Indulgences or additional fruit salad from your daily fruit serves.

> These are very filling and make a yummy meal. Maple syrup uses 15 Optional units per teaspoon – to make it go further, heat it in the microwave.

Food units per serve
1 PR = egg
2 CB = flour
1 D = milk
1 F = peaches

Pixie Biscuits

Serves 15
¼ cup plain flour
8 tablespoons rolled oats
2 tablespoons artificial sweetener
30 g (1 oz) coconut
30 g (1 oz) sultanas
2 tablespoons butter
1 tablespoon golden syrup
½ teaspoon baking soda
3 tablespoons boiling water

1 Mix the flour, rolled oats, sweetener, coconut and sultanas together.

2 Melt the butter and golden syrup.

3 Dissolve the baking soda in boiling water and add to the butter and golden syrup. Make a well in the centre of the flour and stir in the liquid. Lightly spray two baking trays. Place the mixture in spoonful lots on the trays, flattening slightly. Bake at 180ºC for 15-20 minutes.

Food units per serve
60 Optional Indulgences

Strawberry Cookies 'n Cream Delight

Serves 6
8 chocolate wheaten biscuits
185 g (3 oz) strawberry diet jelly
3 teaspoons gelatine
250 ml (8 fl oz) boiling water
1 cup strawberries
250 g (8 oz) smooth cottage cheese
2 tablespoons light sour cream
250 ml (8 fl oz) diet lemonade

Topping
strawberries to garnish
185 g (3 oz) strawberry diet jelly
250 ml (8 fl oz) boiling water

1 Crush the biscuits roughly so that there are some chunky pieces. Sprinkle on the base of a large dish or in the bottom of some parfait glasses.

2 Dissolve one jelly sachet and gelatine in a cup of boiling water. Set aside to cool.

3 Blend the strawberries, cottage cheese and sour cream. Add the jelly and gelatine and blend. Mix in the diet lemonade.

4 Pour the mixture over the biscuits. (The biscuits will float.) Place in the refrigerator to set.

5 Make up the second jelly sachet with a cup of boiling water and cool. Place the strawberries over the set dessert and pour the cooled jelly over the back of a spoon to form a layer over the dessert. Return to the refrigerator until set.

Food units per serve
1 D = cottage cheese
105 Optional Indulgences = strawberry, biscuits, sour cream

Sweet Pumpkin Scones

Serves 12
3 cups self-raising flour
1 teaspoon mixed spice
1 teaspoon cinnamon
1 cup pumpkin, cooked and mashed
1 tablespoon orange zest
250 ml (8 fl oz) low-fat unsweetened yoghurt
65 ml (2 fl oz) soda water

1 Preheat the oven to 200°C.

2 Sift the flour and spices together. Add the pumpkin, orange zest and yoghurt and gently fold into the mixture. Slowly add the soda water to make a soft dough. (Only add as much soda water as is needed – you do not want to make the dough sticky.)

3 Turn the dough onto a lightly floured board. Knead and form 12 scones.

4 Place the scones on a baking tray lightly sprayed with cooking spray. Bake at 200°C for approximately 10 minutes or until golden brown. Serve alone, with diet jam or 100 per cent fruit jam.

Food units per serve
120 Optional Indulgences
or
1 CB = flour
20 Optional Indulgences = yoghurt

Tropical Cheesecake

Serves 4
8 ginger nut biscuits
500 ml (18 fl oz) low-fat milk
2 tablespoons cornflour
4 teaspoons honey
2 egg yolks
1 teaspoon vanilla essence
4 teaspoons gelatine
250 g (8 oz) smooth cottage cheese
juice of ½ lemon
1 teaspoon lemon zest
440 g (16 oz) tinned tropical fruit salad in natural juice, drained

1   Crush the biscuits roughly (there should be some chunky pieces). Sprinkle over the base of a large dish or in the bottom of some parfait glasses.

2   Combine the milk, cornflour and honey. Stir constantly over a low heat until thickened (or microwave for approximately 4 minutes on high). Quickly beat in the egg yolks while the custard is still hot. Cool and add the vanilla.

3   Dissolve the gelatine in 2 tablespoon of boiling water and stir into the custard.

4   Mix the cottage cheese, lemon juice, zest and custard together and blend until smooth. Stir though the fruit salad. Pour over the biscuits and set in the refrigerator.

Food units per serve
1 PR = cottage cheese
1 CB = ginger nuts biscuits
½ F = fruit salad
1 D = milk
60 Optional Indulgences = cornflour, honey, yolks

Vanilla Slice

Serves 9
18 lattice biscuits
750 ml (24 fl oz) low-fat milk
2 tablespoons honey
3 tablespoons custard powder
1 egg yolk
4 teaspoons gelatine
65 ml (2 fl oz) boiling water
4 tablespoons icing sugar
1 tablespoon light sour cream
1 passionfruit

1 Line a container with tin foil. Place 9 biscuits in the container. (If the container size is too big then roll a tea towel and use it to pad against the sides to make the right size container.)

2 Heat the milk, honey and custard powder, stirring constantly until thickened. Remove from the heat and beat the egg yolk through.

3 Dissolve the gelatine in the boiling water and add to the custard mixture. Allow to cool, but do not set.

4 Pour the custard over the biscuits, then layer the remaining 9 biscuits on top. Place in the refrigerator to set.

5 Mix the icing sugar, sour cream and passionfruit pulp. Spread over the top of the biscuits and serve.

This is a yummy treat, but you really need a spoon or fork to eat it!

Food units per serve
180 Optional Indulgences or
1 CB = biscuits + 80 Optional Indulgences

MORE SUCCESS STORIES

Marnie Croft was a size 20 (left) before starting the Weigh Less Naturally program. She lost 30 kilograms and has successfully maintained that loss for two years.

Graeme and Sheryl Kirby before (left) and after the Weigh Less Naturally program. Together, they have now lost 52 kilograms.

INDEX